Meditations on the Birth of Christ

Meditations on the Birth of Christ

Reflections for Advent in the Context of Chinese Culture

YOU BIN

Translated by Johan Ferreira

Foreword by David F. Ford

RESOURCE *Publications* • Eugene, Oregon

MEDITATIONS ON THE BIRTH OF CHRIST
Reflections for Advent in the Context of Chinese Culture

Copyright © 2021 You Bin. All rights reserved. Except for brief quotations in critical publications or reviews, no part of this book may be reproduced in any manner without prior written permission from the publisher. Write: Permissions, Wipf and Stock Publishers, 199 W. 8th Ave., Suite 3, Eugene, OR 97401.

Resource Publications
An Imprint of Wipf and Stock Publishers
199 W. 8th Ave., Suite 3
Eugene, OR 97401

www.wipfandstock.com

PAPERBACK ISBN: 978-1-7252-9855-2
HARDCOVER ISBN: 978-1-7252-9856-9
EBOOK ISBN: 978-1-7252-9857-6

05/14/21

Except where otherwise noted, Scripture quotations are from the ESV® Bible (The Holy Bible, English Standard Version®), copyright © 2001 by Crossway, a publishing ministry of Good News Publishers. Used by permission. All rights reserved.

Contents

Foreword | vii
Preface: Where Is Bethlehem? | xi

PART I: CHRIST IS BORN INTO HISTORY
 1 O Lord, Come! | 3
 2 My Spirit Rejoices in God | 8
 3 The Descendants of Abraham | 13
 4 Serving Him without Fear with Holiness and Righteousness | 18
 5 Let It Be to Me According to Your Word | 25
 6 Conceived through the Holy Spirit | 30

PART II: CHRIST IS BORN INTO THE WORLD
 7 Glory to God in the Highest | 39
 8 My Eyes Have Seen Your Salvation | 45
 9 They Named Him Jesus | 50
10 The Flight to Egypt | 56
11 My Father's Business | 62
12 Prepare the Way of the Lord, Make His Paths Straight | 68
13 The Last Adam | 73

PART III: CHRIST IS BORN INTO US
14 The Poor | 81
15 Those Who Mourn | 87
16 The Meek | 92
17 Those Who Thirst for Righteousness | 99
18 The Merciful | 105

19 The Pure in Heart | 110
20 The Peacemakers | 119
21 Those Who Are Persecuted for Righteousness | 130
    Epilogue: How May Christmas Be Completed? | 138

Bibliography | 141

Foreword

It has been my privilege to know Professor You Bin for over twenty years. During that time I have been increasingly impressed by his academic work in research and teaching; by his leadership—not only in his own university, but more widely, both within and beyond China; by his development of the practice of Scriptural Reasoning in China; and by his collegial relationships and friendships around the world. But until I read these meditations on the birth of Christ I had not read anything he had written about his faith and Christian commitment. It has been deeply moving to do so.

This is a book that embodies a mature Chinese Christianity. It has the depth of mainstream Christianity through two thousand years. It is richly scriptural, with a lively and sensitive interweaving of Old and New Testaments. It draws on classic Christian thinkers, such as Origen, Augustine, Anselm, St. Francis, Bonaventure, Brother Lawrence, St. John of the Cross, and St. Thérèse of Lisieux. It is hospitable to the wisdom of different Christian traditions—Orthodox, Catholic, and Protestant. Yet at the same time it is deeply Chinese, as is shown in the engagement with such thinkers and writers as Confucius, Mencius, Laozi, Lao Tzu, Zhang Zai, Zhu Xi, and Wang Yangming. This is a Chinese Christian wisdom that has much to teach the rest of the world.

The structure of each meditation is well crafted in order to enable readers to go as deeply as possible into each topic.

First, there are short opening quotations from the Bible, which can be meditated upon before anything else.

Then there are some questions. Most of these are the sort of questions that are worth taking through life: you never finish answering them. They remind me of many of the questions Jesus asked, such as his first words to this first disciples in the Gospel of John: "What are you looking for?" Professor You Bin knows that any learning community has to be centered on good questions, and that for us to be disciples (which simply means "learners") we have to be gripped by the great questions of meaning, truth, and wisdom.

Next come the meditations themselves, where one deep topic after another is explored. The three sections, "Christ Born into History," "Christ Born into the World," and "Christ Born into Us," show the breadth of reality within which Professor You Bin thinks and lives. Readers are invited into God-centered living that shapes us into persons more open to God, more open to other people, and more open to the world God loves, including the natural world and its present environmental crisis. We are encouraged to have a scriptural imagination, and to form our lives, our communities, and our societies in line with a worldview that is both indebted to the Bible and ongoing Christian tradition and also responsive to modern life.

Finally, there are short prayers that lead the meditation further into communion with God. Readers who incorporate these into their own pattern of prayer will find that they can be the basis of a well-balanced spirituality. It is a spirituality that is good for beginners but also has the capacity to draw one deeper and deeper.

The title says this book is about the birth of Christ, but in fact it embraces his birth, boyhood, baptism, teaching, transfiguration, passion, death, and resurrection, and also strongly emphasises the work of the Holy Spirit in the life of Jesus and in the lives of his followers.

One context in which I have collaborated with Professor You Bin is that of Scriptural Reasoning. In the Chinese practice of Scriptural Reasoning, in whose development Professor You Bin has played a leading role (especially through being director of the Institute for Comparative Scripture and Interreligious Dialogue, based in Minzu University), texts on a particular topic are chosen from Christian, Muslim, Buddhist, Daoist, and Confucian writings, and then are intensively studied and discussed together in small groups. Professor You Bin is a leading practitioner and has also written extensively on it. Scriptural Reasoning is remarkable in the way it encourages participants to go deeper into their own scriptures and also deeper into the scriptures of others around the table, yet without requiring that that they agree with each other. It has the capacity to foster a healthily plural society. But it only works if each participant first of all goes deeply into the scriptures of his or her own tradition. The meditations in this book show Professor You Bin being deeply and wisely Christian, and they will be a precious gift not only to his fellow Christians but also to

Foreword

anyone else who wants to appreciate better what it can mean to be Christian in the twenty-first century.

David F. Ford
Regius Professor of Divinity Emeritus, University of Cambridge

Preface
Where Is Bethlehem?

Christmas, or the event of "the Word becoming flesh," could be said to be the core of the Christian faith. As the apostle John said, "And the Word became flesh and dwelt among us, and we have seen his glory, glory as of the only Son from the Father, full of grace and truth" (John 1:14). The incarnation determines the Christian understanding towards the holy triune God, human nature, history, and all of life.

Speaking more vividly, Christmas is the birth of the God-man as a baby, born for us. The writers of the gospels used delicate brushstrokes to report the story to us. The story allows us to enter the world of the first disciples, seeing with our eyes, listening with our ears, touching with our hands, and feeling with our hearts: Jesus was born.

The worldwide church has fashioned a long tradition of preparing for Christmas. Every year four Sundays before Christmas, Christians begin to adjust their minds and hearts to the spirit of Christmas. This period is referred to as the season of Advent. This volume provides a series of thematic meditations for the season of Advent in order to immerse ourselves in the Scriptures, allowing us to adjust our minds and hearts step by step to recognize the significance of the birth of Jesus for our lives. As the five wise virgins, who "took oil in their vessels with their lamps" (Matthew 25:4), we use the Word of God as our lamp and our hearts as the oil to wait for the arrival of the Lord.

Through meditation on the Christmas event, each one of us may learn from the example of the shepherds in the fields, who said, "Let us go over to Bethlehem and see this thing that has happened, which the Lord has made known to us" (Luke 2:15). Every Christmas, our hearts may go to Bethlehem in a spiritual sense to see what the birth of this little baby means

Preface

to us and what he has accomplished for us. The story also encourages us to follow the example of Mary, the mother of Christ, who "treasured up all these things, pondering them in her heart" (Luke 2:19). This quiet and thoughtful woman, when God's mysteries had not yet been fully revealed, kept all these things in her heart, like hiding a great treasure, savoring it again and again, and by faith nourished the tree of life.

When we meditate on the Bible and use our hearts to relive the first coming of Jesus into history, we also direct our hearts to the future, looking forward to the second coming of Jesus at the end of the age. We simultaneously open our hearts and invite Jesus to enter our hearts, welcoming him "on this day" of his coming into our lives.

Christ was born in Bethlehem, but where is Bethlehem? If our heart is Bethlehem, then Christ is born into our hearts. We know Jesus when our hearts meet with him. In him we meet the God of heaven and earth. He establishes the realm of our life.

If our life is Bethlehem, then Christ is born into our lives. We follow the principles of life that Christ has established for us, growing in faith, hope, and love; managing our families; and serving him in holiness and righteousness. He is restoring our life and our families.

If our society is Bethlehem, then Christ is born into our society. We establish his church in society. The church is his body. In the journey to the new heavens and the new earth, we expand the body of Christ. He establishes his kingdom for us within our social world.

If our universe is Bethlehem, then Christ is born into our universe. Everything in the universe finds its true meaning in the Holy One who became a man. The Word became flesh, the Creator became a part of the creation, and God sowed in this world a seed that is completely transforming all things. His divine redemptive work, through the sigh of the Holy Spirit in all things, is reviving nature that was impaired by human sin. He leads us together with all things to praise God.

This is how we celebrate and relive the mystery of Christ's birth every year: he is accomplishing an eternal renewal. He is born into our hearts, he is born into our lives, he is born into our society, and he is born into our world.

At Christmas time, there is a birthing of Christ that takes place in each of our hearts; it is our encounter with Christ through the Holy Spirit. In the form of a feast, we are brought into the presence of Christ. We once again come to the fountain and drink the water of life. We come to the light and receive enlightenment.

In this period of Advent, let us come to meet the Word of God and witness the Christmas of Jesus with the New Testament saints.

Like Mary, who said, "My soul magnifies the Lord, and my spirit rejoices in God my Savior" (Luke 1:46–47), let us also demonstrate *joy*.

Like Simon, who said, "Lord, now you are letting your servant depart in peace, according to your word; for my eyes have seen your salvation" (Luke 2:29–30), let us likewise demonstrate *peace*.

Like Mary, who said, "Behold, I am the servant of the Lord; let it be to me according to your word" (Luke 1:38), let us likewise demonstrate *submission*.

Like John the Baptist, who said, "Prepare the way of the Lord, make his paths straight" (Mark 1:3), let us likewise demonstrate *preparation*.

Like Anna, who was "worshiping with fasting and prayer night and day" (Luke 2:37), let us likewise demonstrate *worship*.

The Son of Man who was born in Bethlehem not only moves our hearts, but also wants to cheer our soul and nourish our nature. In these weeks of meditation, we come to Jesus to focus on him and to look at him in faith. "I looked at him, and he looked at me," and in each other's eyes we commune together. In looking at God incarnated, we learn to die constantly to our old sinful self. At the same time, we also pray that the true light "which gives light to everyone" (John 1:9) will illuminate the eyes of our hearts in the light of his gaze and teach us to look at all of life through his truth, integrity, and compassionate eyes.

May the Father and the Son together breathe the Holy Spirit into our lives so that we may share in his nature, love him more, follow him more, and become more and more like him.

You Bin
Beijing

PART I

Christ Is Born into History

1

O Lord, Come!

SCRIPTURE

"O Lord, come!" (1 Cor 16:22 NKJ)

"'Yes, I am coming soon.' Amen. Come, Lord Jesus." (Rev 22:20)

QUESTIONS

1. Why do we focus on the theme "O Lord, come!" during Christmas season?
2. Christ was born in Bethlehem more than two thousand years ago. Why do we still need to cry out "O Lord, come!"?
3. What does the call "O Lord, come!" mean for our personal lives today?
4. From the history of redemption in the Old Testament, how did the Israelites hope for the coming of the Lord?
5. In what ways do all things in the universe exclaim "O Lord, come!"?

MEDITATION

As we prepare for the Christmas season, we adjust our hearts and minds to a short but powerful melody, "O Lord, come!" (*Maranatha*, 1 Cor 16:22).

The prayer for the coming of the Lord has a double meaning. On the one hand, from a liturgical perspective, the season of Advent expresses the hope of the Lord's coming. It uses the liturgical calendar to remember the coming of the Lord Jesus two thousand years ago. On the other hand, the season of Advent also encourages us every year to look forward to the second coming of the Messiah, just as the Israelites in the Old Testament did. This prayer reminds us of our intermediate identity (or dual identity). The Lord has already come in history and his coming into the world has enabled us to know God and to become God's children. At the same time, as God's children, we hope that he will return on the last day to bring heaven and earth together and to gather the people of the world into his eternal kingdom. Like Abraham, we are still travelers, embarking on the journey of hope. But Jesus has already been born, giving deep roots to our hope. From the testimony of Jesus' birth, we are already members of the new covenant, but according to the hope of Christ's second coming, we are like the members of the old covenant.

"O Lord, come!" This is not just a simple prayer; it is a cry of hope from the depths of our hearts, from history, and from nature.

Firstly, it is a cry to the Lord from the depths of every soul. Humanity was made by God, and God placed his image in the depths of every person's heart, and so naturally the human heart reflects the glory of the triune God. God breathed his divine nature into human life, and so the human heart can find true rest only in fellowship with God. Exclaiming "O Lord, come!" is but a cry for God to come into his own place, to occupy our hearts as his own dwelling. The birth of Jesus fulfilled God's plan of salvation in human history. The future of our salvation also lies in his coming, but it requires our work by means of prayer, preparation, and hope. The cry "O Lord, come!" is the alarm bell that opens our hearts.

Secondly, it is also the shout of Israel from the depths of history to the Lord. Ever since the sin of our first ancestors and their expulsion from paradise, it has become the eternal hope of humanity to overcome evil and to live again with the Lord in paradise. In his judgment upon evil—personified by the serpent—the Lord God prophesied: "The descendant of the woman will crush your heart" (Gen 3:15). Later, God called Israel out of all nations and made a covenant with their fathers—Abraham, Isaac, and

Jacob—to raise up "the blessing of all nations" (Gen 12:3) from among their descendants. In the events of the exodus from Egypt, God's presence with the Israelites was symbolized by the pillar of cloud and the pillar of fire. God even let his glory reside in the tabernacle of the people of Israel, thereby living among them. However, Israel's life in the promised land was a history of failure: internally, they could not escape their own sinfulness, and externally, they continued to suffer the prolonged bullying of other powerful nations. Their hope for the Messiah was manifested in the proclamation made by generations of prophets, from the prophecy of the prophet Isaiah, "The virgin will be with child and will give birth to a son, and will call him Immanuel" (Isa 7:14), to the words of the last prophet, Malachi, "See, I will send my messenger, who will prepare the way before me. Then suddenly the Lord you are seeking will come to his temple; the messenger of the covenant, whom you desire, will come, says the Lord Almighty" (Mal 3:1). The hymn of Mary and Zechariah represents the expectation of Abraham and the house of David. The cry "O Lord, come!" echoes the voice of all Israel.

Finally, it is also the cry of the whole created world to the Lord. The world God had originally created was harmonious and beautiful, but the relationship between human beings ruptured when our first ancestors disobeyed God's command. Since humanity and the world are both created by God and are intrinsically connected, the sin of the first humans not only led to humanity's expulsion from paradise, frailty, and suffering, it also affected the entire created order. "Cursed is the ground because of you" (Gen 3:17); the earth that provided fruit and vegetables for humanity now "will produce thorns and thistles" (Gen 3:18). In the days of Noah, because "the Lord saw how great man's wickedness on the earth had become, and that every inclination of the thoughts of his heart was only evil all the time" (Gen 6:5), God judged humanity through a great flood, the whole created order was also implicated. Again, as the prophet Hosea said, "There is only cursing, lying and murder, stealing and adultery; they break all bounds, and bloodshed follows bloodshed. Because of this the land mourns, and all who live in it waste away; the beasts of the field and the birds of the air and the fish of the sea are dying" (Hos 4:2–4). Therefore, the battered and bruised land also sends out the deep cry of hope, yearning for salvation from heaven, "O Lord, come!" In the near future, our hearts, together with all things in heaven and earth, will hear and join in the cheers emanating from the universe, as sung in the book of Psalms: "Let the sea resound, and everything in it, the world, and all who live in it. Let the rivers clap their hands, let the mountains sing together for joy; let them sing before the Lord, for he comes to judge the earth. He will judge the world in righteousness and the peoples with equity" (Ps 98:7–9). The prayer "O Lord, come!" is the cry of all things in the world to their Creator.

In the coming three weeks of Advent, meditating on the birth of the Lord is both a memorial to the Lord's first coming as well as an expectation of his second coming. In the first coming, the Lord Jesus was clothed in linen and placed in the manger; in the second coming, he will be clothed in glory and riding the clouds. In his first coming he was despised and crucified; in his second coming he will be revealed in power with numerous angels. We are living in an intermediary time. Through meditating on his first coming, we are waiting for his second coming. The constant refrain through the passage of time is the cheering voice of the disciples of the New Testament: "Blessed is the king who comes in the name of the Lord!" (Luke 19:38; Matt 21: 9; John 12:13)

"O Lord, come!" We welcome you!

PRAYER

O Lord God, Immanuel, come! Redeem your people. We wander here alone after being expelled from your garden, waiting for your coming.

Come, you are wisdom from heaven! The things that are near and far are determined by you, show us the Word of your truth, teach us the way of life.

Come, you are the Lord of Might! You appeared on the holy mountain of Sinai amid the cloud and fire; you gave Israel your law. Illuminate us with your pillar of fire and lead us by your pillar of cloud.

Come, you are the new branch of Jesse's root! Save all those who trust in you from the hands of your enemies, may they overcome the threat of death and give birth to new sprouts of life.

Come, you are the key of the house of David! Open for us the door of our heavenly home, pave the way to highest heaven, where there are no longer sighs of sorrow and pain.

Come, you are the daylight that comes from heaven in the morning! Dispel the clouds of darkness and welcome us to your side. The shadow of death sees you and flees.

O Lord, Come!

Come, you are the longing of all nations! The heart of humanity unites because of you, pacify all disputes and quarrels, let the peace of heaven fill this world.

Lord, we want you to come!

Amen.

2

My Spirit Rejoices in God

SCRIPTURE

"And Mary said, 'My soul magnifies the Lord, and my spirit rejoices in God my Savior . . .'" (Luke 1:46–47)

"Rejoice in the Lord always; again I will say, rejoice." (Phil 4:4)

QUESTIONS

1. What was so special about Mary's situation when she composed her hymn to the Lord?
2. Why was Mary so joyful? Where does her joy come from? What kind of mental state does her hymn reflect?
3. Why do our hearts experience true joy only when we magnify the Lord?

MEDITATION

In Luke 1:46–55 there is a hymn that was sung by Mary. Christian tradition has named the hymn after its opening word, *Magnificat*. It is the first of four famous hymns in the Gospel of Luke; the other three are: the *Benedictus* by Zechariah (1:67–79), the *Gloria in Excelsis Deo* by the angels (2:13–14), and *Nunc Dimittis* by Simeon (2:28–32). This collection constitutes Luke's compilation of praise for the birth of the Lord. The *Magnificat* is one of the most important hymns in the history of the church. It is a direct reflection of Hannah's joyous hymn in 1 Samuel 2:1–10, and almost every sentence corresponds to passages in the Law, the Prophets, and the Writings. But when it was finally written, it formed a seamless hymn. It is often used in the daily devotion of the evening or morning prayer service. The Catholic and Orthodox Churches as well as Protestant denominations attach great importance to this poem.

The first line of the hymn, **"My soul magnifies the Lord, and my spirit rejoices in God my Savior,"** is the crowning crescendo of the entire song. We cannot help but ask: What is the reason for Mary's joy? What is the source of Mary's joy?

The reason why we raise this question is because Mary's joy here is obviously not derived from sensory pleasure; it is a transcendent joy that does not depend on external circumstances and it brings about inner blessedness and spiritual tranquility. In the social structure of ancient Israel, kings, priests, and prophets were the elites of society. In the time of the New Testament, in the Jewish synagogue the scribes who explained the scriptures to the people also became the intellectual elites among the Jews. However, Mary does not belong to any of these classes; she is just an ordinary woman within Jewish society. Therefore, the question regarding Mary's joy is also addressed to us: What kind of spiritual realm may an ordinary Christian experience and enjoy?

Feng Youlan, a twentieth-century Chinese philosopher, once divided humanity's spiritual state into four levels or realms: the natural realm, the utilitarian realm, the ethical realm, and the universal ("heaven and earth") realm. The person in the natural realm is a "natural person." In this realm people are totally subjected to their own biological nature and have no spiritual life that a free and independent person should possess. The person in the utilitarian realm is a "utilitarian" who only cares about personal success, which is to strive for fame and gain as the goal of all pursuits. A human in the ethical realm is a "moral person" who knows right and wrong, who can constrain instinctive impulses with standards of good and evil, and who abides by socially recognized moral rules. The person in the "heaven and earth" realm is a "universal human being," which means that his or her heart is in harmony with the original essence of the universe and enjoys spiritual harmony in union with the essential principal of the universe. In fact, Mary's praise in the *Magnificat*, "My soul magnifies the Lord," refers to the joy that God's people have reached after spiritually entering into the realm of "heaven and earth." It tells us that even an ordinary person like Mary, regardless of position or education, as long as there is a proper relationship with God in heart and mind, can reach the heights and depth of "heaven and earth."

Mary's joy in the Lord is a portrayal of the realm of heaven and earth that every Christian can possess. In fact, in Luke's gospel, when Mary sang this hymn she was at a special moment in time. First, she submitted her will to God's plan and aligned her life with God's plan. At first, when the angel announced to her that she would conceive and have a child from the Holy Spirit, Mary was greatly disturbed. She asked, "How can this be?" (Luke 1:34), but she soon added, "Behold, I am the servant of the Lord; let it be to me according to your word" (Luke 1:38). She accepted in her heart the mission that God had arranged for her and willingly agreed to be an instrument of God's purpose determined before the creation of the world. Secondly, Jesus had been conceived in her and the Lord was with her (Luke 1:42). Finally, Mary, being moved by the Holy Spirit in concert with Elizabeth, who was also filled with the Holy Spirit, revealed her joy to the world (Luke 1:41). In fact, these three factors—obeying God's will from the heart, Christ in us, and the guidance of the Spirit—determine the Christian's attitude towards life. Therefore, Mary's joy in the Lord should also become the spiritual realm that every Christian is to possess, appreciate, and expand.

Mary's joy does not consist in making God the object of joy, because if so it would only use God as an external object and would reduce the joy of heaven and earth to a general cognitive or aesthetic activity. The metaphor of Christ being within the womb is most appropriate for expressing Christian joy as reunification with God. With faith we receive the salvific grace of Christ in the inner person by the Holy Spirit and so each one carries the shape of Christ. As Ephesians states, "Let Christ dwell in your heart through your faith" (3:17). When Christ is formed in our hearts (Gal 4:19), the mystery of Christmas is once again fulfilled in each one of our hearts. Through Christ as our intermediary, we are again united with our heavenly Father. This is what Christ meant when he said, "I am in the Father, and you are in me, and I am also in you" (John 14:20).

Mary "rejoices in God." Where does her joy come from? The answer is implied in the first sentence of her hymn: "My soul magnifies the Lord..." According to the parallelism of ancient Israelite poetry, the two sentences correspond to each other: "my soul" corresponds to "my spirit," and "rejoices in God my Savior" corresponds to "magnifies the Lord." Then, what does it mean to magnify the Lord?

We may ask: How does the soul magnify the Lord? The Lord does not need our praise. He is what he is, and we cannot add anything to the Lord, nor can we detract anything from the Lord. But our hearts are created in the image of Christ, and each of us is shaping our heart so that it reflects Christ's image to varying degrees. Therefore, in different people's hearts, the image of Christ is either large or small, dark or bright, dirty or clean. In this way, when we use our minds and thoughts, actions, and activities to magnify the Lord in us, it is actually making the image of the Lord bigger in our hearts, and so our hearts will share the image of God and make it become bigger and cleaner. If we continue to sin, our hearts will become smaller and dirtier, and so the image of the Lord will become smaller and more blurred in our hearts. Further, if we create other idols in our hearts and honor them, then we also take on the appearance of the devil and no longer reflect the image of Christ. It can thus be seen that to "magnify the Lord" is not to increase the Lord's glory but is constantly to restore and cleanse our own hearts, and so to adjust our spiritual direction to enter the principle of life which is the basis of the universe.

Our heart is based either on "magnifying the Lord" or using other created objects as idols of life. In the final analysis, it is the question of whether we can distinguish the worthy from unworthy, and treasure from rubbish. Most people make the pursuit of wealth the goal of life, but for Christians who are interested in rejoicing in God there are things more lovely and desirable than wealth. The name of God is referred to as "holy," that is to say, God's power is far above all created things. He should be the *big* one of the human heart to love and to desire. In contrast, the external fortunes of life—wealth and rank, longevity and brevity of life, and health problems—are all *small*. When Mary can see the *big* one, she naturally forgets the *small* one. In magnifying the infinitely big God, Mary has been able to expand her own heart and realize a high degree of security, fulfillment, and happiness. In this sense, the joy of Mary, an ordinary woman, is fulfilling the Chinese ideal for the spiritual life: "In heaven and earth there are many noble things that may be loved and pursued. A person should pursue the greater things and ignore the smaller things. If you set your heart on the greater things, your heart will be serene and content. When there is no discontent, your heart will feel the same, whether rich or poor, noble or humble."[1] That is to say, the heart can be united with the one who is greatest, and so is able to be content. For those who are content, riches and poverty are all the same. Even if you live in an alleyway or live on crude tea and simple food, you cannot change the joy of being in communion with God.

The reason why Mary's *Magnificat* is continually being sung in churches today is because it asserts that every ordinary Christian can have and should pursue the realm of faith that lies beyond all external fortunes. Nothing in the world will be able to influence and affect the highest joy of those who magnify the Lord in the heart. This joy is brought to them by the realm of heaven and earth, which does not depend on any external thing, but relies only on the world set up in the heart. There, the faithful meet with the Lord of the universe.

PRAYER

Christ, you are our heavenly joy. We pray that you unite us with you in faith so that you may become our joy.

We pray that we can rely on the power of the Holy Spirit in our lives, always full of hope, and that we never lose your joy in us.

Oh Lord Jesus, in accordance with the deep love of God, you have accepted us as we are. We pray that you will give us the strength to accept each other, and to share the joy of the heavenly family in your love.

Oh Lord Jesus, we pray that you would sanctify the chosen ones, accept the ones who look upon you, and help all who are needful, so that we can all share in eternal blessings and happiness.

Amen.

---

1. Zhou, *Penetrating the Book of Changes*, 38.

3

The Descendants of Abraham

SCRIPTURE

"The book of the genealogy of Jesus Christ, the son of David, the son of Abraham . . ." (Matt 1:1)

"Now the LORD said to Abram, 'Go from your country and your kindred and your father's house to the land that I will show you. And I will make of you a great nation, and I will bless you and make your name great, so that you will be a blessing. I will bless those who bless you, and him who dishonors you I will curse, and in you all the families of the earth shall be blessed.'" (Gen 12:1–3)

QUESTIONS

1. How did the incarnation of Jesus fulfill God's promise to Abraham that "in you all the families of the earth shall be blessed"?
2. What is the spiritual significance of tracing the beginning of the genealogy of Jesus back to Abraham in the Gospel of Matthew?

MEDITATION

The opening statement of Matthew's gospel is also the introduction to the entire New Testament. It is a long family tree of Jesus. Why does the gospel begin in this way? A genealogy tells where a person came from. Understanding a person's origin enables us to understand his or her mission and what he or she will do. Jesus' genealogy in Matthew's gospel seems to describe his past but it is a statement about his future mission. It is also an in-depth echo of the genealogical narratives in Genesis, thereby linking the birth of Jesus in the New Testament with the theme of salvation of humanity and the universe in the Old Testament.

In the Old Testament tradition, the family tree is a special literary genre. On the surface, the genealogy simply records who has given birth to whom. However, through the use of a genealogy, a person's origin can be traced back to the most distant past, even to the first person, the world's creation, and so on. The genealogy describes the relationship between descendants, ethnic groups, and families, whether far or near, light or heavy, mainstream or marginal. Every civilization with a long history pays close attention to genealogies. The position of people in the genealogy not only reflects their position in society, but also reflects how they understand their historical mission.

In the Pentateuch of the Old Testament, the genealogy provides the basic background for God's plan of salvation. The book of Genesis follows a well-known genealogical structure: after every section of history an important genealogical story appears. In the Hebrew text, the role played by the family genealogy is expressed by the word *toledot*, with the root of *dly*, however Chinese versions of the Bible have used different words to translate it. For example, Genesis 1 is about the creation of the universe, so in Genesis 2:4 we read, "These are the generations [*toledot*] of the heavens and the earth when they were created, in the day that the Lord God made the earth and the heavens." Chapter 3 tells the story of Adam and Eve being punished after eating the forbidden fruit. Then in Genesis 4:1 we read, "Now Adam knew Eve his wife, and she conceived and bore [*dly*] Cain." After that we have the story of Cain's killing of Abel. Next, in Genesis 4:17 there appears another birth story, which is a family story from Cain. Afterwards, we have the story of Lamech. Then in Genesis 5:1 the narrative begins to talk about Adam's *toledot*, a genealogical story of Adam from Seth. Afterwards, we have the story of Noah and the flood. Then in Genesis 10:1 the genealogy (*toledot*) of Noah is given. Afterwards, there follows the story of the tower of Babel. People attempted to build a tower that reached the sky to promote humanity's own name, but the outcome was that God confused human language and so people scattered to form the different nations of the world. In Genesis 11:10–26 the genealogies (*toledot*) of Noah's sons appear, until the birth of Abraham. From then on, Abraham continues the genealogical narrative: in Genesis 25:19 we have the descendants of Isaac and in Genesis 37:2 the descendants of Jacob.

Genesis uses genealogy to connect its entire native. It is not only a simple literary technique, but it has profound spiritual and theological implications. Firstly, it means that the history of humanity and even of the whole universe is under God's control. God's will is unfolding in the history of humanity from generation to generation. Moreover, in the history of humanity certain families or groups have special significance; they are the instruments through whom God accomplishes his plan of salvation in history. Their genealogy is the red line God has laid down in history. Secondly, these ever-expanding yet narrowing family narratives, as a constantly focusing lens, tell people how God's grace continually falls on specific characters. Finally, it also makes us realize that the family or individuals who are under the historical lens of the genealogy participate in God's mission of salvation not only for themselves, but also for their larger family, and in fact for the entire human race and creation.

The author of Matthew's gospel was a person who studied the Old Testament writings in depth. When he wanted to write a gospel to describe the meaning and mission of Jesus' coming into the world, he naturally chose the literary device of the genealogy. Jesus' family tree began with Abraham, but it also connects to the story of Abraham's forefathers, Seth, Noah, and Adam, and even to the creation of heaven and earth. Its purpose is to tell people that Jesus' mission is to continue God's saving action since Abraham for humanity and creation, as "all the families of the earth shall be blessed" (Gen 12:3).

The genealogy of Jesus in Matthew begins with Abraham. This forms an echoing relationship between Jesus and Abraham. It reminds us that to understand Jesus' mission we must return to God's promise in Abraham's initial call: "in you all the nations of the earth shall be blessed" (Gen 12:3). Abraham was called by God from among the nations and went to the promised land. His mission had three important elements: to become a great nation, to have many descendants, and to be a blessing to all nations. This means that among Abraham's descendants a special figure would be born who would reverse the situation in which the people of the nations were scattered because of the Babel turmoil. All the nations would be reunited and gathered before God through Abraham's descendant.

The history of the Israelites did not fulfill God's promise to Abraham. At the end of the Old Testament era, the Israelites fell under the new power around the Mediterranean world. Israel became a Roman colony. As people of one of the smallest nations on the east coast of the Mediterranean, the Israelites were very weak. Belief in one God, the Creator of heaven and earth, was also mainly confined to the Israelites and was not widely disseminated. The promise that "in you all the nations of the earth shall be blessed" seemed to be unfulfilled. But God's promise did not stop there; through the power of the Creator, he arranged the birth of Jesus. When people had lost faith about Israel's mission of salvation, God wonderfully fulfilled the promise of Abraham's call.

Jesus was born from the blood of the Israelites. The line from Abraham, David, Zerubbabel, and Joseph and Mary delineates his lineage in the world. But the purpose of his birth was not only for Israel but for the salvation of all people. People were originally created in the image and likeness of God, but because of Adam's sin, they fell into injustice and death. Later, humanity became even more depraved and departed further away from God. People were scattered throughout the earth after Babel; nation competed with nation, and humanity became God's enemy. God chose Abraham to make him and his descendants a blessing to all people. This was also to restore God's blessing to humanity, which was the original purpose of creation (Gen 1:28). God's promise to Abraham crossed the long period of Old Testament history until it was finally fulfilled in the birth of Jesus. This blessing is that the people of all nations can become the covenant people, just as the Israelites, and through Jesus Christ, the "first-born of creation," be restored into the image and likeness of God. In Christ the people of all nations are being united into one. Regardless of differences in language, color, or culture, they all belong to the people of heaven. They form the church, which is the sprout and beginning of the kingdom of heaven on earth, which is indeed the "great nation" of the Abrahamic promise (Gen 12:2).

PRAYER

Lord, since you have been born into the world, we welcome the coming of your kingdom.

You once called Abraham to gather your children. We pray that you remember your children on the earth and fulfill the promise you made to Abraham.

May you give us the faith of Abraham to journey to the heavenly city you have prepared for us.

Lord, we pray that you make us a great nation in Christ, as you promised to the ancestors: one body, one soul, and one people. Protect your church; she is the people of the new Israel.

Amen.

4

Serving Him without Fear with Holiness and Righteousness

SCRIPTURE

"That we, being delivered from the hand of our enemies, might serve him without fear, in holiness and righteousness before him all our days." (Luke 1:74–75)

"There is no fear in love, but perfect love casts out fear. For fear has to do with punishment, and whoever fears has not been perfected in love." (1 John 4:18)

"So the law is holy, and the commandment is holy and righteous and good." (Rom 7:12)

QUESTIONS

1. Since God saved us from the bondage of sin, what kind of life does he demand from us?
2. How should Christians live in the world?
3. What position with God enables us to live before him with peace and assurance?

4. According to the Bible, what does "holiness and righteousness" mean? Or what is a holy and righteous life?

MEDITATION

This first verse above is part of Zechariah's hymn. Zechariah was the father of John the Baptist. He was a priest in the temple of Jerusalem and was very familiar with the spiritual traditions of Israel. Being filled with the Holy Spirit, he sang this hymn and prophesied about the role that John and Jesus would play in the salvation of Israel and of all humanity. Although the words are short and refined, the meaning is very far-reaching. Since the hymn is filled with many allusions to the Old Testament, it is difficult to understand the spiritual significance of Zechariah's praise without an understanding of the Old Testament.

In short, the verse "that we, being delivered from the hand of our enemies, might serve him without fear, in holiness and righteousness before him all our days" alludes to the two traditions of exodus and Sinai in the books of Exodus and Leviticus. The hymn uses the spiritual connotations of the deliverance of Israel and the establishment of the covenant to describe the life that Jesus Christ will bring to humanity.

The spiritual meaning of this verse may be understood and contrasted with two passages in Exodus. The first one is Exodus 3:12. After the Lord God appeared to Moses, he called on him to perform a great mission: "When you have brought the people out of Egypt, you shall serve God on this mountain." The other passage is Exodus 19:4-6. "You yourselves have seen what I did to the Egyptians, and how I bore you on eagles' wings and brought you to myself. Now therefore, if you will indeed obey my voice and keep my covenant, you shall be my treasured possession among all peoples, for all the earth is mine; and you shall be to me a kingdom of priests and a holy nation." Living a holy life means obeying God's word, as Paul said: "the law is holy, and the commandment is holy and righteous and good" (Rom 7:12). Therefore, in the New Testament hymn of Zechariah, the major themes of the Old Testament are combined: deliverance from Egypt and the establishment of the covenant at Sinai, salvation and service, freedom and the keeping of the law.

We may say that Zechariah's hymn recalls the two most important traditions of the Old Testament and uses them to answer the following questions: What kind of life should Christians who have been saved by the incarnation of Christ now live? According to what criteria should they live? The exodus enabled Israel to be free. God saved his people out of the slavery in Egypt so that they could serve him in freedom. It was also to enable people to enjoy freedom in serving him.

When Zechariah sang this hymn, it was a turning point in the history of salvation. At that time, just when John was born and Jesus was about to appear, the Word of God was to become human and live among people. Therefore, Zechariah's hymn, echoing the exodus and Sinai traditions in the Pentateuch, also particularly emphasizes that Jesus' salvation would bring a huge difference to the way people relate to God. This is what he sang in his hymn: "that we, being delivered out of the hand of our enemies, might serve him without fear" (Luke 1:74).

In the book of Exodus, after decisively escaping their enemies through the crossing of the Reed Sea, the Israelites arrived before God at Mount Sinai. In their experience of the presence of God, in the closeness of intimacy, they "beheld God, and they ate and drank" (Exod 24:11). But more often than not, God met the people in thunder, lightning, and dense clouds, which resulted in fear, terror, and trembling (Exod 19:16; 20:18). In the Old Testament era, the *shekinah* glory of God, God's presence with the Israelites, expressed both the grace of God to the Israelites as well as his hiddenness, reminding them of the distance between God and humanity. However, in the New Testament era, the God of infinite blessings, to save humanity in a mysterious way that surpasses human understanding, entered the human sphere in infinite closeness through the Word becoming flesh. The conception and birth of Jesus would bring about complete salvation and would change the state of fear that people experience in the presence of God. Those who accept Jesus as Savior will come into God's presence in a state of freedom, peace, and selflessness. This ability to "serve him without fear" is determined by the threefold identity of God's people.

Their first identity is as the "children of God." The Son became flesh and died on the cross to enable people to share his identity of sonship. This status allows us to call the almighty Creator of the universe "Father" when we pray and say, "Our Father, who is in heaven." We are no longer "slaves" and are no longer afraid of God. The third person of the Trinity, the Holy Spirit, assures us that we have received the heart of a true child of God by accepting the name of Jesus, so we can boldly and fearlessly come to God and call him "Abba, Father!" (Eph 3:12; Rom 8:15).

Furthermore, because of Jesus' incarnation, the new status of sonship we acquire is not just an adjustment of title but indicates a substantial change in nature. In Jesus Christ, we have "become partakers of the divine nature" (2 Pet 1:4). As the ancient church father Irenaeus, bishop of Lyons (c. 130–202), said, God has "become what we are, that He might bring us to be even what He is Himself."[1] The Holy Spirit moves us and forms Christ in our hearts to become the children of God, not only metaphorically but actually; something has changed in the heart of Christians; a new divine life has been birthed.

Christians' second identity is as "lovers of God" (2 Tim 3:4). Christians are usually regarded as people who believe in God (believers of God), but at a deeper level "faith" refers to a relationship of love, and so Christians may more accurately be described as "lovers of God." Love is not just an action, nor just an attitude, but rather an ongoing state of reality. In the interaction between God and humanity, only the verb "love" is used interchangeably with respect to both God and people. Therefore, I prefer to use the expression "God's lover" rather than the expression "people who love God." The letter of 1 John has an excellent description of Christians as lovers of God, living in the wonderful realm of God's love: "And so we know and rely on the love God has for us. God is love. Whoever lives in love lives in God, and God in them. This is how love is made complete among us so that we will have confidence on the day of judgment: In this world we are like Jesus. There is no fear in love. But perfect love drives out fear because fear has to do with punishment. The one who fears is not made perfect in love" (1 John 4:16–18).

The loving relationship with God has truly opened a realm of life for Christians that transcends good and evil. Because love is a power in the following way: the law of love is love itself. It does not care what it will be, what it is, or what can be done. Love does not think, love does not consider, love does not evaluate. Love is driven by itself. Love ignites desires and drives toward the forbidden and the impossible.

A classic model of "God's lover" is the "sinful woman" who washed Jesus' feet with her tears (Luke 7:36–50). Love for Jesus, like big waves, drowns the fear of the sinner before God. Love compels her to the Lord; she is driven to embrace Jesus; love makes her brave enough to enter the meeting of the Pharisees without fear; love makes her speechless and she is immersed in intimate contact with Jesus.

---

1. In Roberts and Donaldson, eds., *Writings of Irenaeus*, 1:351–52.

The Christian's third identity is as "God's friend." In the Bible, as a specific title, the expression "friend of God" is only used to describe Abraham and Moses (Isa 41:8; also see Exod 33:11). "And the scripture was fulfilled that says, 'Abraham believed God, and it was credited to him as righteousness,' and he was called God's friend" (Jas 2:23). Since Abraham became God's friend through faith, all who have a relationship with God through faith in Jesus Christ can also be called the "friends of God" in the broad sense. So, what is a friend? In interpersonal relationships, "My friend is not another person, but my other half. Therefore, I must regard my friend as myself. Although my friend and I have two bodies, within the two bodies, there is only one heart."[2] In short, a friend is a person of the same heart, a "second me." Christians can be called the "friends of God" by keeping their own hearts in the Holy Spirit and through communion with God's heart; they know each other from the depths of their spirit. In the heart of every individual, there is the image of God. Even after original sin, though the image of God has been blurred, it has not been eliminated. Jesus Christ was the original image of God, and everything, including our inner being, was made through him. He became incarnate and took the human form to restore the human image of God. After a person becomes a Christian, the image of Christ enters his inner heart. When we act with integrity and holiness, we are displaying the image of Christ in the light of glory; when the image of Christ is exalted, our inner image also shares his glory and greatness. Sharing the same heart of friendship is indeed the portrait of this relationship between Christ and us.

To have a life of calmness and fearlessness before God is a portrait of the Christian's realm of life in fellowship with God. However, the second part of Zacharias's hymn defines the way in which people demonstrate fellowship with God in the realm of life, that is, in serving him "in holiness and righteousness." What does "holiness and righteousness" mean here? Is there any scriptural evidence in the Bible that enables us to understand what these terms mean? As mentioned earlier, Zachariah's hymn is a hymn that stems from the depths of the history and spirit of the Israelites. Therefore, to understand its specific connotations, we still need to turn to Old Testament revelation to find the answers.

Romans 7:12 says, "So then, the law is holy, and the commandment is holy, righteous and good." Therefore, in short, to "serve him . . . in holiness and righteousness" means to serve him according to the law. After

---

2. Ricci, "Treatise on Friendship," 107–8.

the exodus, the Israelites obtained freedom not to indulge their sinful passions, but freedom to come to Sinai to make a covenant with God, who said, "Now if you obey me fully and keep my covenant, then out of all nations you will be my treasured possession" (Exod 19:5). Although the laws that Moses and the Israelites obtained in Sinai were varied and complex, their essence consisted in "holiness and righteousness." Christians who have a new covenant with God through Jesus Christ also need to live according to the Law as a guide to life. Therefore, Jesus also said, "Do not think that I have come to abolish the Law or the Prophets; I have not come to abolish them but to fulfill them. For truly I tell you, until heaven and earth disappear, not the smallest letter, not the least stroke of a pen, will by any means disappear from the Law until everything is accomplished" (Matt 5:17–18).

The spirit of "holiness and righteousness" pervades every article of the Mosaic Law from Exodus to Deuteronomy. Generally speaking, we could divide it according the five levels of the Christian life. Firstly, it is state of mind in which people realize that "the Lord is my God" and know that they belong to the Lord God. Between the Christian and God there is an intimate relationship that knows that "my beloved is mine and I am his" (Song of Songs). Secondly, it is reflected in family relationships, like honoring parents, respecting the elderly, faithfulness in marriage, loving your siblings, and treating children well. Thirdly, it is embodied in fair and just social relationships, like fairness in court cases and honesty in business transactions. In the book of Leviticus we read, "You shall do no wrong in judgment, in measures of length or weight or quantity. You shall have just balances, just weights, a just ephah, and a just hin. I am the Lord your God, who brought you out of the land of Egypt" (Lev 19:35–36). The wages of the hired workers cannot be withheld overnight (Lev 19:13). Fourthly, it is also manifested as giving for the poor and sojourners. Many statements in the Law of Moses remind us of this responsibility; for example, in Leviticus we read, "When you reap the harvest of your land, you shall not reap your field right up to its edge, neither shall you gather the gleanings after your harvest. And you shall not strip your vineyard bare, neither shall you gather the fallen grapes of your vineyard. You shall leave them for the poor and for the sojourner: I am the Lord your God" (Lev 19:9–10). It is necessary not only to share wealth, but also to preserve the dignity of the poor. Finally, it is also reflected in treating the environment and other living things well. The Law of Moses stipulated the institution of the Sabbath and the Jubilee year. "But in the seventh year there shall be a Sabbath of solemn rest for the land, a Sabbath to the Lord. You shall not sow your field or prune your vineyard. You shall not reap what grows of itself in your harvest, or gather the grapes of your undressed vine. It shall be a year of solemn rest for the land. The Sabbath of the land shall provide food for you, for yourself and for your male and female slaves and for your hired worker and the sojourner who lives with you, and for your cattle and for the wild animals that are in your land: all its yield shall be for food" (Lev 25:4–7). These five dimensions can also be used to summarize Paul's statement in Galatians: "For you were called to freedom, brothers. Only do not use your freedom as an opportunity for the flesh, but through love serve one another. For the whole law is fulfilled in one word: 'You shall love your neighbor as yourself'" (5:13–14).

This line of Zechariah's hymn, which reflects the Old Testament's revelation on how people stand before God, has opened the New Testament implications about how people enjoy the freedom of being in Christ. Its spiritual content is very deep and broad.

PRAYER

God became flesh and lived among us. God of Immanuel, please give us hope and joy in you.

Lord, you came to the world not for judgment but to call your people who had gone astray. Your love nurtures all creatures, and your mercy embraces the whole world.

You look upon us with your love, and in your gaze of love, we are fearless.

Lord, you released us from the bondage of sin; may you lead us in your ways with the light of truth. Empower our hearts with your love to fulfill your holy and just commandments.

May we stand before you without fear and in peace, when you come again with the power and glory.

Amen.

5

Let It Be to Me According to Your Word

SCRIPTURE

"And he came to her and said, 'Greetings, O favored one, the Lord is with you!' . . . And Mary said, 'Behold, I am the servant of the Lord; let it be to me according to your word.'" (Luke 1:28, 38)

"I am again in the anguish of childbirth until Christ is formed in you!" (Gal 4:19)

QUESTIONS

1. How did Mary respond to God's call?
2. In light of Mary's response to God's gracious call, what transformation will Christians experience in their lives?
3. "Let it be to me according to your word." What does Mary's response mean for us today?

MEDITATION

At that time, God's plan of salvation, which had been set in place before the creation of the world, was about to unfold in the world. When his Word was to enter human history, God prepared a woman, a descendant of Eve, to realize the plan of the incarnation. This woman was Mary. The Gospel of Luke introduces Mary in the following way: "In the sixth month the angel Gabriel was sent from God to a city of Galilee named Nazareth, to a virgin betrothed to a man whose name was Joseph, of the house of David. And the virgin's name was Mary" (1:26–27).

The woman chosen by God, whether we consider the Roman context or the Jewish context, was very ordinary. At that time, Israel's religious and cultural center was in Jerusalem, in Judea in the south, whereas Galilee was some distance to the north and Nazareth was just an average village. People did not believe that any prophet would come from Nazareth, let alone the Messiah. Mary and Joseph were an everyday couple struggling to make ends meet. Joseph worked hard to make a living with his skills as a carpenter. God's choice of Mary to accomplish his plan of salvation illustrates his omnipotence as Creator. A little speck of dust, being illuminated by God's light, can indeed become a blessing to the entire world. In fact, Mary's call by God and her being filled with the Holy Spirit is a picture of every ordinary Christian today. The realization of God's plan in each individual has nothing to do with his or her status, wealth, or knowledge. Listening to God's call and responding to it in the heart means entering into a covenant relationship with the God who created the universe.

The central figure in God's salvation is Jesus, but Mary's role in God's plan of salvation is special. Jesus did not experience the trials that led up to his birth and the anguish that followed his death, but Mary experienced it all. Mary was the only person who was present both when Jesus was born and when he died. She saw his birth as a baby and also witnessed his death on the cross. What greater joy could there be than hearing the annunciation of the birth of the Son, sharing the news of divine conception with Elizabeth, seeing the birth of Jesus in the manger, attending the presentation of the baby in the temple, and discovering the boy Jesus discussing the scriptures with all the scholars in the temple? But, on the other hand, what greater sadness could there be than hearing the prophecy regarding Jesus' death by Simon, fleeing to Egypt to escape the massacre of Herod, losing her beloved son in the temple, meeting Jesus carrying the cross on the way to Golgotha, seeing her son being crucified, then holding the dead body of her son and laying it in the tomb? Mary was an ordinary woman, but as the story of Jesus unfolds, the emotional experiences of her heart reflect our human experience in the world. Even if people do not fully experience her deep-seated emotional turmoil, her joy and sorrow, even in the smallest matters of life, Mary's experience may arouse people's inner thoughts and feelings.

Let us focus our meditation on Mary's inner thoughts and feelings when the angel spoke to her the following words: "Greetings, O favored one, the Lord is with you!" (1:28), and: "And behold, you will conceive in your womb and bear a son, and you shall call his name Jesus" (1:31). This is the spiritual journey that every Christian has to walk when he or she hears God's call.

We can imagine that God, who created and chose Mary for his purposes of salvation, who sent Gabriel to announce the news of the incarnation, would not need to consult with Mary, and she just the same would have conceived miraculously the holy one in her womb. However, in accordance with his own will, and proactive love for people, God wants the willing response of individuals. God created people in his own image and endowed them with freedom in order that they may know him and love him. When God, out of love, moves people's hearts, knocks on the doors of their hearts, he expects that people will respond eagerly. It is only in freedom that the human spirit can enter the communion of love. The story in Luke 1:26–38 describes a lengthy dialogue between the archangel and Mary. After the angel announced God's call to Mary, the angels, and the whole world, were all calmly watching and waiting for the response of Mary.

Mary's place in God's plan of salvation is special. All people from Adam were waiting for her reply. Adam and Eve were waiting. Abraham and David were waiting. All people in the land were waiting. The eternal Word of God, through the agreement of her heart and mind, expressed by the verbal obedience of her mouth, would become flesh. Only through this process of the Word becoming flesh can we be recreated and become new people in eternal life. And then through God's electing grace Mary's heart responded through the prompting of the Spirit, "Behold, I am the servant of the Lord; let it be to me according to your word" (Luke 1:38). The consent from her heart brought sunshine to all who sat in the shadow of darkness, release to all who were bound, and hope to all who were poor. Expressed in plain language, it means, "May your will be done!" Mary's decisive response was simple, but its significance is huge. She used a human mouth to express a word, but in her heart accepted the Word of God; she exhaled a brief utterance but accepted the eternal truth; she spoke out a soft sound, but within herself she conceived Christ, the Son of God.

Mary's response to God's call was ordinary. But it is the response of all sinners hearing God's message of salvation, and it is also the response of all Christians who hear God's call on their lives. If a sinner is willing to open his or her heart with the same words when hearing the gospel of God, the expression "your will be done" is the most significant thing in all creation. As Augustine said, "The justification of a sinner is greater than the work of creating the heavens and the earth,"[1] because heaven and earth are going to pass away, but the justification and salvation of his chosen ones will last forever. Every time when God's call comes upon a person's life, God is looking for the willing response of the heart: "Behold, I am the servant of the Lord; let it be to me according to your word." Through this response from the heart, God's sovereignty and human freedom interact to build a new world.

Mary's obedient response from the depths of her heart was a turning point in her life. She opened her mouth and issued a declaration of obedience; she opened her heart and accepted grace from above; she offered her body and allowed Christ to be conceived in her. Mary's reply also illustrates the transformation in the life of Christians when they respond to God's call with obedience. It incorporates three basic elements: believing from the heart, confessing with the mouth, and conception (new life) in the body. When the grace of God comes upon a person, like Mary, it is based on the will of the Father and the coming of the Holy Spirit. When we believe in our heart and confess with our mouths, we receive Christ's salvation (Rom 10:10). Apart from conceiving Christ in our hearts, what also may we conceive? According to the flesh, Christ has only one mother, Mary; but spiritually speaking, all of us, like Mary, conceive Christ in us by faith. This is what Paul said in Galatians 4:19: "I am again in the anguish of childbirth until Christ is formed in you!" If we are not able to live according to the law of Christ, which is love, nurturing our Christian virtues, Christ will not mature in us and we will only be weak and incomplete.

Mary's "Behold, I am the servant of the Lord; let it be to me according to your word" also illuminates our meditation on the relationship between God's grace and human freedom. God's call to humanity in grace is unconditional, stemming entirely from God's freedom and initiative. His calling goes beyond the rational understanding of human beings and also beyond the resolve of one's own will, because, as the Creator of all things, the will of God transcends the power of all creatures. However, when God touches the soul through the operation and illumination of the Holy Spirit, a person is

---

1. Thomas Aquinas, *Summa Theologica*, I-II, q. 113, a. 9

not completely passive. He or she can accept or agree, but he or she can also resist or oppose. Like Mary, people can consent to God's call and election. This consent does not mean that Mary added her own ability or willingness to complete God's grace; rather her response was only the action of emptying herself and willingly accepting the work of the Holy Spirit, allowing him to perfect the work that he began in her.

"Let it be to me according to your word." This is the first step in the Christian life, Christ in us and we in Christ. From then on, "It is no longer I who live, but Christ who lives in me" (Gal 2:20). But it is not only the first step; it is also repeated throughout our lives as we are taking the pilgrimage towards the heavenly city. All over the world the hearts of people continue to respond to the Lord's call with the words, "Let it be to me according to your word," in order to head for perfection, to live with God, and to act in his love.

PRAYER

The Holy Word descended and became flesh; the Word of the Lord was fulfilled in his humble servant. We earnestly pray, Lord live in us now.

Your words are the life power of the universe, according to your command. Everything emerged from nothingness. Use your word to bring your new creation to completion in our hearts.

You called in your Word to the lost sinner: "Where are you?" Use your Word to call sinners and give them new and eternal life.

You used your Word to proclaim the law of new life to your people. Now give us the light in your Holy Word, to lead our feet along the way of peace.

Holy Lord, may your Word be fulfilled among us, that we may share the divine life of Christ, walk in his love, and welcome his second coming with joy.

Amen.

6

Conceived through the Holy Spirit

SCRIPTURE

"Now the birth of Jesus Christ took place in this way. When his mother Mary had been betrothed to Joseph, before they came together she was found to be with child from the Holy Spirit." (Matt 1:18)

"And the angel answered her, 'The Holy Spirit will come upon you, and the power of the Most High will overshadow you; therefore the child to be born will be called holy—the Son of God.'" (Luke 1:35)

QUESTIONS

1. How does Mary's conception of Jesus through the Holy Spirit relate to the birth of our new Christian life?
2. How does the Son and the Holy Spirit cooperate in God's plan of salvation?
3. How does the Holy Spirit produce Christ's life in us?

Conceived through the Holy Spirit

MEDITATION

The short texts in the two gospels quoted above reveal the inseparable relationship between the Holy Spirit and the Son in the decisive salvific event of the incarnation. It also anticipates that in every Christian new life will be produced and nourished by the Holy Spirit until it is fully grown and mature.

The incarnation of Jesus is the result of the joint action of the triune God. The idea of the triune God that Christians believe in may be expressed as: the Son in the Father with the Holy Spirit. Worshiping any one of the persons includes the other two. God himself is not an absolute single entity but there is a relationship of love and communion between the three persons. The statement "God is love" (1 John 4:16) means t not just that love is a function of God, but in an ontological sense it is another expression of the Holy Trinity. Because God exists in three persons, God is love. At the same time, because God is love, God exists in three persons. Every person of the Godhead is fully divine and is presenting himself as a gift to the other two in a constant and perfect relationship of love. The Father is the source of the Holy Trinity. He gives his richness fully to the Son and the Holy Spirit. The Son and the Spirit return their love to the Father, and at the same time they exchange love and fellowship with each other so that an unbroken unity is formed between all the persons of the Holy Trinity. The trinity is theologically referred to as a "community" (*perichoresis*). In the work of God's redemption, the Holy Trinity always works in unison from beginning to end.

The moment Mary became pregnant, when the Word took on flesh, the cooperation between the Holy Spirit and the Son was intimate. On the one hand, the Holy Spirit added his own mission to the mission of the Son, obeying the call of the Son, and cooperated with the incarnation of the Son. On the other hand, the Holy Spirit, as the life-giving Lord, sanctified the womb of Mary and transformed the Word of God into flesh to become an ordinary person with soul and body as we have. In ancient church tradition, the birth of Jesus from the womb of the virgin Mary and the generation of the Son from the Father before the creation of the world constitute a corresponding relationship: "Before all ages, there was no mother, and the Son was born to the Father; in the last age, with no father, Jesus was born to Mary."[1]

---

1. "Sermon 196" in Rotelle, ed., *Works of Saint Augustine*, 6:60.

The work of the Holy Spirit is evident in the work of the Son by Mary becoming pregnant. Prior to this, the Holy Spirit also shared in the mission of the Son in a hidden way. Firstly, in the original creation, the Holy Spirit moved over the chaos and gave birth to all things. The Father exhaled the Spirit, together with the Son, who is the first image of the Father, and created all things. The Holy Spirit acts as God with the Father and the Son. He gives life to the creatures of creation, manages them, and sanctifies them. In humanity's creation, the Holy Spirit and the Son are like the hands of the Father, giving the tangible person the image of God. It is precisely because the Creator breathed the Holy Spirit into the nostrils of the human form that the human became a "living being" (Gen 2:7) who was capable of forming a relationship of knowledge and love with God.

Secondly, in the history of salvation, the Holy Spirit continually revealed to the prophets that the Son was coming into the world. In the "first gospel," right after our first ancestors, Adam and Eve, were expelled from paradise, the Redeemer is promised: "I will put enmity between you and the woman, and between your offspring and her offspring; he shall bruise your head, and you shall bruise his heel" (Gen 3:15). In the call of Abraham, which commenced a new beginning in the history of salvation, all people on the earth will be blessed through the descendent of Abraham (Gen 12:3). The essence of prophecy is that the Holy Spirit revealed to the prophets the coming of the Son. The Holy Spirit revealed to the prophet Isaiah, "Therefore the Lord himself will give you a sign. Behold, the virgin shall conceive and bear a son, and shall call his name Immanuel" (Isa 7:14). In the Songs of the Suffering Servant in Isaiah (Isa 42:1–4; 49:1–6; 50:4–9; 53:1–11), the Holy Spirit inspired the prophet to predict that Jesus was indeed the Suffering Servant and that through his suffering and death he would give us the Spirit of life.

Finally, fundamentally speaking, the preparation and proclamation of the birth of the Son of God is also the work of the Holy Spirit. Before the Word became flesh, the Holy Spirit was involved in the conception of John the Baptist, who was "filled with the Holy Spirit, even from his mother's womb" (Luke 1:15). When Mary went to visit Elizabeth, we heard the Holy Spirit's greetings and praises to the Son. "And when Elizabeth heard the greeting of Mary, the baby leaped in her womb. And Elizabeth was filled with the Holy Spirit, and she exclaimed with a loud cry, 'Blessed are you among women, and blessed is the fruit of your womb!'" (Luke 1:41–42). John's mission in the world was to witness and prepare the way for Jesus.

John was the culmination of the Old Testament prophets, because he spoke directly to the Savior prophesied in the Old Testament. In John, the Holy Spirit fulfilled the prophecies he revealed through the Old Testament prophets. The prophecy that John the Baptist made when he baptized Jesus was exactly what the Old Testament prophets had envisaged. "And John bore witness: 'I saw the Spirit descend from heaven like a dove, and it remained on him'" (John 1:32).

At the decisive moment of God's salvation, Christ was conceived by the Holy Spirit and became a physical body. But after the resurrection, Christ sent the Holy Spirit and nurtured Christ's new life in everyone who received him. As Paul says in Ephesians 3:17, "so that Christ may dwell in your hearts through faith—that you, being rooted and grounded in love . . ." Every Christian begins to have faith because of the work of the Holy Spirit. In this sense, the expression that Mary "was found to be with child from the Holy Spirit" is a picture of every Christian. Through faith, the Holy Spirit conceives Christ into every believer so that "Christ is formed in you" (Gal 4:19). This miraculous conception that must take place in the bosom of every Christian is generated by the Holy Spirit. Similarly, it needs the guidance, nourishment, and presence of the Holy Spirit to grow and to mature.

This is another example of the cooperation between the Son and the Spirit in the redemptive work of the Father. In the first instance, Mary conceived the Son through the Spirit; in the second instance, the Son sent the Holy Spirit to produce his life in us. In the first instance, it was the incarnation: God became man; in the second instance, it is *theosis*: humanity comes to participate in the divine nature through the power of Holy Spirit. Humanity may now share in the life of communion and harmony of the Trinity. The first instance addressed the general nature of humanity, so that people may be rescued from the power of sin and death. The second instance addressed everyone, so that the individual may obtain unique and eternal life. The Holy Spirit communicates the perfectness of divinity to everyone in a unique, individual way. The Holy Spirit is the giver of life and is the endless source of life. He is not depleted by the large number of people he shares with, nor is he diminished by being shared. He is everywhere and in everyone. Everyone shares the life of Christ because of him. Everyone's life is different. He is like the sun; people enjoying the sun seem to enjoy it alone, but the sun shines on the whole earth at the same time, shining on the sea and enlightening the sky. The Holy Spirit gives common grace to all people, yet he is only for those who receive him.

In this sense, we can understand the significance for the Christian life of Mary becoming pregnant by the Holy Spirit. Mary was pregnant with a child, the Holy Spirit conceived the Son in her, without destroying the integrity of her body. Her chastity was intact. When Christians receive Christ's life from the Holy Spirit, their external physical and social identities do not change, but they have a new inner life. This inner life is like a treasure hidden in jars of clay; although the outer body of the person is withering away, the inner person is renewed day by day (see 2 Cor 4:7–16).

Under the influence of the Holy Spirit, the life of Christ grew in the womb of Mary. Then, for today's Christians, where is Mother Mary's womb? This is the church. The ancient church father Cyprian (d. 258) stressed, "If you do not take the church as your mother, you cannot have God as your Father."[2] This emphasizes not only the authority of the church, but also the role of the church as a believer's spiritual mother. The Holy Spirit's nourishment and sanctification are infused into the life of believers through the church's sacred word and sacraments.

The Holy Spirit conceived Christ in our lives. He also requires us to relive all of Christ's life in us. Under the power of the Holy Spirit, we have become one with Christ. This requires us to continue, practice, and live out the example and teachings of Christ. Sharing the life of Christ, living out the form of Christ, and bearing the fruit of the new life in the Holy Spirit; this is the universal meaning of being conceived through the Holy Spirit for each one of us.

PRAYER

Lord Jesus, you are the Messiah who was anointed by the Holy Spirit. Save us.

At the beginning of creation, your Holy Spirit hovered over the waters and incubated all living things. May your Spirit descend upon us and breathe eternal life into us.

In accordance with the Father's will, you were conceived and nurtured by the Holy Spirit in Mary's womb. We pray that you recreate us in your word, your flesh and blood, through the same Spirit, that we may share in your divine life.

---

2. Cyprian of Carthage, *On the Unity of the Church*, sec. 6.

Conceived through the Holy Spirit

In the waters of the Jordan River, the Holy Spirit descended upon you as a dove. May your Spirit also descend upon us and pour forth in us the living water that will never run dry.

Amen.

PART II

Christ Is Born into the World

7

Glory to God in the Highest

SCRIPTURE

"And suddenly there was with the angel a multitude of the heavenly host praising God and saying, 'Glory to God in the highest, and on earth peace among those with whom he is pleased!'" (Luke 2:13–14)

"'Peace be within your walls and security within your towers!' For my brothers and companions' sake I will say, 'Peace be within you!' For the sake of the house of the Lord our God, I will seek your good." (Ps 122:6–9)

QUESTIONS

1. How does this verse describe the state of harmony and joy between heaven and earth when Jesus was born?

2. In the Old Testament, how was the integration of heaven and earth realized? What change did Jesus' incarnation bring in the relationship between heaven and earth?

3. The church is called the "the body of Christ." How can Christians in today's church receive the blessing and joy that heaven and earth have in common?

MEDITATION

Among the four major hymns at Jesus' birth in the Gospel of Luke, this hymn, which is traditionally known as the *Gloria*, is the shortest, yet its meaning is most significant. It reveals the relationship between heaven and earth in the understanding of the Christian faith.

Due to some minor variations in the wording of the hymn in various ancient manuscripts, there are slightly different understandings of its meaning. The footnote in the Chinese Union Version of the Bible specifically makes this point: "Some manuscripts read: 'Joy to all people.'" The problem lies in the last Greek letter of the hymn. If there is one more letter "s," it defines the previous word, "people," which then means "the people with whom he is pleased." The current meaning of the Chinese Union Version expresses this idea. If there is one letter less, then it is a noun, meaning "joy," juxtaposed with the previous glory and peace. According to this understanding, the hymn reads: "Glory to God in the highest place; on the earth there is peace, and among people there is joy."

No matter how we understand the details, the basic meaning is the same: Jesus' birth means the coming of the heavenly Savior to the earth. He brings harmony and joy to heaven, to earth, and to humanity. From the perspective of heaven, Jesus' incarnation came from God's management of the world and manifests God's omnipotence and mercy, for which the angels honor God. From the perspective of the earth, the advent of Jesus Christ saved the world from the bondage and oppression of sin, and thus all things experience harmony. From the perspective of humanity, in the Word becoming flesh people could receive the salvation of God in Christ, be reconciled to God, and experience unspeakable joy in the heart. In Jesus Christ, heaven, earth, and humanity are restored to their proper place; they are united in the sound of praise and the universe is filled with peace, joy, and blessing.

Because of Jesus' incarnation, this blessed harmony between heaven, earth, and humans became possible. Christ is the Word of God. He has the same essence and dignity as God. He is the image of first life since creation. Everything was created through him. But out of God's incredible love and almighty power, Christ became flesh and was born in Bethlehem and laid in a manger. This Christ who lived on earth is fully divine as well as fully human. In him, heaven, earth, and people can be brought together, and each receive blessing, hence there is glory in heaven, peace on earth, and joy among people.

Heaven and earth are united, and humanity rejoices. This is the main theme and purpose of salvation history since Adam and Eve were expelled from the garden of Eden after the commencement of original sin. People were very eager to receive the grace that comes from heaven to earth. When Abraham was called to go to the promised land, he built an altar and called on the name of the Lord in every place he settled. Jacob also often met with God in different places, for example in Bethel, where he saw angels ascending and descending on a ladder reaching into heaven. When Moses fled to Midian, he experienced God's call in the fire of the burning bush at Sinai. He then led the Israelites out of Egypt and the whole nation witnessed the appearance of God on Mount Sinai. God also instructed Moses and the Israelites to build the ark of the covenant and the tabernacle. After that, the tabernacle became the "portable" Sinai. The tabernacle became a place where heaven and earth met and where people could receive God's forgiveness through the ceremonies God ordained.

After the Israelites entered the promised land, in the time of Solomon, the temple was finally built on Mount Zion. In Solomon's prayer at the dedication of the temple, we read, "I have indeed built you an exalted house, a place for you to dwell in forever" (1 Kgs 8:13). The temple was where heaven and earth met, and where people rejoiced in God. The temple is said to be the "navel" of heaven on the earth. The prayers of the people on the earth in the temple would be heard by God. As Solomon prayed, "Yet have regard to the prayer of your servant and to his plea, O Lord my God, listening to the cry and to the prayer that your servant prays before you this day" (1 Kgs 8:28–29).

Many psalms speak about the temple; it is the place where the angels give glory to the Lord. "Ascribe to the Lord, O heavenly beings, ascribe to the Lord glory and strength. Ascribe to the Lord the glory due his name; worship the Lord in the splendor of holiness" (Ps 29:1–2). It is a place on earth where people may enjoy peace and joy. "How precious is your steadfast love, O God! The children of mankind take refuge in the shadow of your wings. They feast on the abundance of your house, and you give them drink from the river of your delights. For with you is the fountain of life; in your light do we see light" (Ps 36:7–9). The temple is also a place where people's hearts are secure and jubilant. "Though an army encamp against me, my heart shall not fear; though war arise against me, yet I will be confident. One thing have I asked of the Lord, that will I seek after: that I may dwell in the house of the LORD all the days of my life, to gaze upon the beauty of the Lord and to inquire in his temple" (Ps 27:3–4).

Given this spiritual context of the Old Testament, we can understand the significance of the *Gloria* in the Gospel of Luke when the shepherds, accompanied by a heavenly host of angels, worshiped God. When Christ became incarnate, his body became "the house of God" (John 2:18–21). When he appeared in the flesh, the shepherds, the angels, and the heavenly hosts sang together, "Glory to God in the highest, peace on earth, and joy among people." This was exactly what happened in the temple worship in the Old Testament, where heaven, earth, and people came together in unison.

However, today's Christians can no longer be like the shepherds in Luke's gospel, standing beside the newly born Jesus in blissful harmony with heaven and earth singing "glory to God in the highest." Where then can we go to find this place of glory in heaven, peace on earth, and joy among people? After the resurrection of Christ, his body continues to exist in the world in another form, which is the church.

Based on the incarnation of Christ, the church represents a union between heaven and earth, a community or a place where there is a combination of the divine and the human. The church is both human and divine; it is visible and invisible; it works in the earth and yet raises its heart to pray to heaven; it places itself in the world and goes to the heavenly land (Heb 11:16). To say that the church is the body of Christ is not just a metaphor. The church is not only centered around Christ but is united with him as his body. The brothers and sisters that Christ calls from all peoples through his holy Word form his mysterious body; and believers "eat his flesh and drink his blood" in Holy Communion, so that Christ dwells in believers and believers also in him. Christ is the head of the church, the church is the body of Christ, and Christ and the church together constitute a holistic Christ.

In the church, we can see, hear, and touch the Christ that was born in Bethlehem. Similarly, just as the shepherds in the gospel witnessed the spiritual reality of the Word becoming flesh, today's Christians can also be united with heaven, earth, and people in harmony and joy in the church.

Firstly, the church is a place where all the saints are united. When the church on earth worships and praises, the saints of heaven are like the clouds around us and together give glory to God in the highest. The liturgies of church worship unite humanity with heaven, or more properly speaking, the children of God on earth join with angels and saints in heaven's everlasting praise.

Secondly, the church also brings peace to the earth. The church is a place of peace and harmony. It is a ship that opens the sail of the Lord's cross and steadily sails through the world under the wind of the Holy Spirit. It is the place of peace where people can be rescued from the flood as in Noah's ark.

Finally, the church also brings joy to people. The church is the instrument and channel through which God shares grace with others. Through the gift of the Holy Spirit, every believer receives the salvation of Christ on the cross and enjoys the dignity of God's free children and can call the Creator of heaven and earth "Abba, Father!" Joy is one of the most prominent characteristics of Christians, and as Paul said: "Rejoice in the Lord always; again I will say, rejoice" (Phil 4:4).

In the Christian belief system, the church unites heaven, earth, and humanity under the headship of Christ. It covers the area meant by the traditional Chinese expression "all under heaven." In Christ, all within the four seas are brothers, because, as Paul says, "There is neither Jew nor Greek, there is neither slave nor free, there is no male and female, for you are all one in Christ Jesus" (Gal 3:28). It also transcends the traditional Chinese expression "all under heaven" because it refers to angels and saints who are united with the triune God in heaven. In the church, believers, benevolent people who love God and others, are integrated with heaven and earth and all things around the triune God; they share in the supreme beauty, peace, and joy.

PRAYER

Lord Jesus, you who are the eternal Word of God before all ages were born for us in time. We extol you! May all heaven rejoice, and may the earth be filled with joy, for you have come!

Lord, you nourished the earth with the nectar of joy. We beseech you to care for us always and to give us joy from heaven.

You are the king of peace between heaven and earth. You sent angels to declare peace to humanity; we beseech you to keep us in your ultimate peace.

Lord, you planted a vine of life on the earth. We pray that you will continue to pour out the Holy Spirit, so that our branches will be closely knit together and produce the fruit of benevolence and peace.

Amen.

8

My Eyes Have Seen Your Salvation

SCRIPTURE

"Lord, now you are letting your servant depart in peace, according to your word; for my eyes have seen your salvation that you have prepared in the presence of all peoples, a light for revelation to the Gentiles, and for glory to your people Israel." (Luke 2:29–32)

"That which was from the beginning, which we have heard, which we have seen with our eyes, which we looked upon and have touched with our hands, concerning the word of life—the life was made manifest, and we have seen it, and testify to it and proclaim to you the eternal life, which was with the Father and was made manifest to us." (1 John 1:1–2)

QUESTIONS

1. What does it mean to see the salvation of God? How does humanity long to see God's salvation?

2. In the history of the Old Testament, how did God's salvation appear to the Israelites?

3. How did God's salvation enter a new stage with the coming of Jesus? What was it that the apostle John and his compatriots "have heard . . . seen . . . and have touched . . . concerning the word of life"?

MEDITATION

According to the Law of Moses (Lev 12), the newborn baby Jesus was brought into the temple and received circumcision. Joseph and Mary also offered sin offerings in accordance with Jewish rituals to cleanse the mother of the new baby. On such an occasion, Simeon saw Jesus and sang a hymn that became famous in the history of the church, known as the "Hymn of Simeon" (or *Nunc Dimittis*, "Now dismiss").

Who is Simeon? What does he represent? Does his hymn have any special significance for our meditation on the advent of the Lord? According to the Gospel of Luke, Simeon "was righteous and devout, waiting for the consolation of Israel, and the Holy Spirit was upon him" (2:25). Because of the words "Lord, now you are letting your servant depart in peace, according to your word" (2:29), people speculate that he would have been an elderly man of great wisdom, who waited for the "consolation of Israel." His hymn, on a personal level, expressed his desire from the depths of his heart to see the face of God, and, on the community level, expressed Israel's hope from the depths of history to see their "Comforter" and "Savior." Only in light of the deep individual experience and the earnest community desire for salvation can one understand the serenity, peace, and satisfaction of Simeon after seeing Jesus. It is precisely because of this that the Hymn of Simeon has been traditionally used in church prayers at the end of the day to prepare for satisfying and peaceful sleep.

What is the "seeing" of God's salvation? Seeing is sharing and possessing. It is the communion of the human soul with God and angels in life and love, and it is the ultimate realm of supreme happiness.

Seeing God's salvation is the deepest desire of humanity since Adam. Humans were created in the image of God. Then they were placed in the garden of Eden and lived with God. However, Adam and Eve violated God's command and suffered the punishment of being expelled from paradise. Since then, people's hearts exist in a state of deep contradiction. On the one hand, the human heart seeks naturally to rest in God: "Your face, Lord, do I seek" (Ps 27:8). If a person cannot rest in God, the heart does not feel safe. On the other hand, in this banished world, people's hearts are often drawn to idols created by human hands. By their own ability, fallen people cannot come to God. Anselm (1033/4–1109), a well-known medieval theologian, described this human dilemma as follows:

> Speak now, my whole heart; speak now to God: I seek Your countenance; Your countenance, O Lord, do I seek. So come now, Lord my God, teach my heart where and how to seek You, where and how to find You. If You are not here, O Lord, where shall I seek You who are absent? But if You are everywhere, why do I not behold You as present? But surely You dwell in light inaccessible. Yet, where is light inaccessible? Or how shall I approach unto light inaccessible? Or who will lead me to and into this light so that in it I may behold You? Furthermore, by what signs, by what facial appearance shall I seek You? Never have I seen You, O Lord my God; I am not acquainted with Your face. What shall this Your distant exile do? What shall he do, O most exalted Lord? What shall Your servant do, anguished out of love for You and cast far away from Your face? He wants to see You, but Your face is too far removed from him. He desires to approach You, but Your dwelling place is inaccessible. He desires to find You but does not know Your abode. He longs to seek You but does not know Your countenance. O Lord, You are my God, and You are my Lord; yet, never have I seen You. You have created me and created me anew and have bestowed upon me whatever goods I have; but I am not yet acquainted with You. Indeed, I was made for seeing You; but not yet have I done that for which I was made.[1]

Therefore, people's desire to seek God is expressed when they turn to divine grace through supplication and prayer. As Anselm said:

> When will You look upon us and hear us? When will You enlighten our eyes and show us Your face? When will You restore Yourself to us? Look upon us, o Lord; hear us, enlighten us, reveal Yourself unto us. Restore unto us Yourself—without whom we fare so badly—so that we may fare well. . . . Permit me, at least from afar or from the deep, to look upwards toward Your light. Teach me to seek You, and reveal Yourself to me as I seek; for unless You teach me I cannot seek You, and unless You reveal Yourself I cannot find You. Let me seek You in desiring You; let me desire You in seeking You. Let me find You in loving You; let me love You in finding You.[2]

Since the fall of humanity into depravity, humanity's sinful nature has plunged people into all kinds of injustices and suffering. It is God who, out of his mercy and compassion, takes the initiative and reveals himself to

---

1. Anselm, *Complete Philosophical and Theological Treatises*, 90–91.
2. Anselm, *Complete Philosophical and Theological Treatises*, 92.

humanity (theophany) and enters human history. He protects the world because of his love and in his grace invites humanity to return to him, embracing the guilty one with compassion. He decided to choose Abraham so that in him "all the families of the earth shall be blessed" (Gen 12:3). In Abraham's experience, God appeared to him many times and he constantly received God's blessing. In his regular experience of God's active manifestation, Abraham also learned not to be afraid of God, but to love him and to be close to him. Jacob also constantly experienced the manifestation of God. As he left Bethel in the promised land, he saw angels ascending and descending on the ladder, and when he was about to return to the promised land, at Peniel he saw God "face to face" (Gen 32:30).

God took the initiative and revealed himself to humanity. In the Old Testament, God's presence with humanity reached its peak in Israel's exodus from Egypt. After Israel was delivered from Egypt, God led Israel through the wilderness with a pillar of cloud during the day and a pillar of fire during the night. At Mount Sinai, God made a covenant with the Israelites. Since the Israelites were to leave Mount Sinai, God set up the ark and the tabernacle and filled the tabernacle with his glory cloud, thus indicating that he would always be present with the Israelites.

In these events, God manifested his salvation in such a way that human eyes could see it. He showed his presence with people by means of cloud and fire. However, these manifestations were incomplete and fearful. Even Moses, who talked to God like a friend, when he requested to see God's glory, got the answer: "you cannot see my face, for man shall not see me and live . . . and you shall see my back, but my face shall not be seen" (Exod 33:20, 23). When God manifested his deep love, people saw only a little glimpse of it.

Prayer to God from the heart is inspired by the flame of God's love. Desiring to meet God face to face, longing to be enlightened by the light of God, longing to see the glory of God with their own eyes—these prayers of the prophets of the Old Testament were answered by the baby who was embraced by Simeon. Simeon said, "My eyes have seen your salvation." He emphasized "my eyes" to show that he saw the "face of God." It was not like the dreams of Jacob, nor like the angels of Abraham. The Word had become flesh and was "heard, . . . seen with our own eyes, . . . and touched with our own hands" (1 John 1:1). There was no longer dread and trembling in God's presence; God's glory was no longer shrouded in "thunders and lightnings and a thick cloud" (Exod 19:16). The Son, like us, ate and drank, and also experienced emotions like ours, including joy (Luke 10:21) and sadness (John 11:35). He became a man such as we are so that we may be like him and be partakers of the divine nature, to be in communion of the eternal life and blessing with the Holy Trinity.

The Hymn of Simeon is full of serenity, peace, and contentment, because with Jesus in his arms he saw the face of God and the inaccessible light. It was the glory that Moses was forbidden to see. When Simeon held Jesus, he enjoyed the sight of God and experienced God's love, compassion, and omnipotence. Before this no one could see the greatness and glory of God and survive. But because of God's love and omnipotence, "With man it is impossible, but not with God. For all things are possible with God" (Mark 10:27). He was actually holding God, who could be heard with the ears, seen with the eyes, and touched with the hands, by those who feared him. How great is this joy and contentment!

PRAYER

Lord, we are waiting for your coming, as at the time of your incarnation; we praise you. You are the invisible true light, the image of firstborn by whom all things were created, who for our salvation became a man. Let us behold you and follow you.

Shine you face upon us and bless us. Turn towards us and give us peace. Let us live each moment of our lives in your light and serve you with our lives.

Reveal yourself to us and let us seek you and know you in all things.

You are the true light that Simeon and the righteous were expecting. Guide our feet into the way of peace as the dayspring from on high has visited us.

Amen.

9

They Named Him Jesus

SCRIPTURE

"And the angel said to her, 'Do not be afraid, Mary, for you have found favor with God. And behold, you will conceive in your womb and bear a son, and you shall call his name Jesus. He will be great and will be called the Son of the Most High. And the Lord God will give to him the throne of his father David, and he will reign over the house of Jacob forever, and of his kingdom there will be no end.'" (Luke 1:30–33)

"But to all who did receive him, who believed in his name, he gave the right to become children of God." (John 1:12)

QUESTIONS

1. The angel said his name would be Jesus. How does this name proclaim his mission?
2. Why does the Bible say that the name of Jesus is above all names (see Eph 1:21; Phil 2:9)?
3. In prayer, how should we address Jesus? How does prayer in Jesus' name sanctify our lives?

MEDITATION

In Christianity, the Word becoming flesh is not just a doctrine of theology, it is a real event. This event allows everyone to enter into a living relationship with God. It is a direct "face to face" relationship between God and humanity, because at the other end of the relationship there is a personal name. God is love, but this divine love has a human name: Jesus.

A name is more than just a sign. In ancient Hebrew thinking, there is a close relationship between a person's name and his or her whole being. The existence of a person, including his or her characteristics and abilities, mission, and work, all exist in his or her name in some way. Therefore, naming a person indicates a special kind of relationship in which two people know each other. In the Hebrew tradition, the name represents the entire existence of a person. To do something in the name of someone, or to call upon his name, is a particularly important and decisive act. Calling on the name of a person makes him or her concrete in time and space.

Luke recorded how the name Jesus was spoken for the first time. This name did not stem from a person's idea or judgment. It was announced by an angel and originated from the hidden depths of the universe. Before the birth of Jesus, the name already existed. In fact, it existed before the creation of the world, because it was derived from God's eternal purpose, as we read in Ephesians, "even as he chose us in him before the foundation of the world, that we should be holy and blameless before him. In love he predestined us for adoption as sons through Jesus Christ, according to the purpose of his will" (Eph 1:4–5). This name revealed the concealed will of God's management of the world. In this name, God's revelation reached the highest point, it summed up the entire history of salvation.

The word "Jesus" in Hebrew means "God saves." In the annunciation, the angel uses some words rooted in Israel's history to describe Jesus' identity and mission. This includes two specific titles: "the King of Jacob's house" and "David's throne." It also includes two more lofty and universal missions: he will be called "the Son of the Most High" and "of his kingdom there will be no end." The first two expressions emphasize that Jesus would fulfill God's promises to the forefathers of the Israelites in the Old Testament, Abraham, Jacob, and David. As king, he would establish a free and peaceful kingdom on the earth in which there would no longer be slavery. The latter two expressions more profoundly mean that Jesus would save people from their sins and provide forgiveness. Through his birth, his divinity was combined with his humanity. Jesus became a man in order that our human nature may be transformed to become the children of God, and to inherit eternal life and blessing from him.

Jesus not only is the sacred name that can bring salvation, but it also reflects the longing of the human soul to call on God with a personal name. After Adam and Eve were expelled from the garden, people longed to see the face of God and to call on his name. Although every person has the knowledge of ultimate consciousness and eternal being engraved in their heart, different religions or cultures express the ultimate reality of the universe through various beliefs and actions such as worship, prayer, or praise. However, only after God revealed himself in the way of a name, and after giving this name concrete meaning through his works in nature and history, could people call upon God and establish a living, face-to-face relationship with him.

Under the call of God, Abraham went to the promised land and began a new stage in God's plan of salvation. But during the time of the ancestors Abraham, Isaac, and Jacob, God appeared to them only as "Almighty God." "I appeared to Abraham, to Isaac, and to Jacob, as God Almighty, but by my name the Lord I did not make myself known to them" (Exod 6:3). Not until God's entry into the history of Israel in liberating them from Egypt did God reveal his holy name to Moses and the Israelites (Exod 3:13–15):

> Then Moses said to God, "If I come to the people of Israel and say to them, 'The God of your fathers has sent me to you,' and they ask me, 'What is his name?' what shall I say to them?" God said to Moses, "I Am who I am." And he said, "Say this to the people of Israel, 'I am has sent me to you.'" God also said to Moses, "Say this to the people of Israel, 'The Lord, the God of your fathers, the God of Abraham, the God of Isaac, and the God of Jacob, has sent me to you.' This is my name forever, and thus I am to be remembered throughout all generations."

This was the first time that God revealed his special name (the Lord; Hebrew: *Yahweh*) to humanity. Through this name, God established a one-to-one relationship with his people Israel. Since then, in the unfolding of the plan of redemption in the history of Israel, the name *Yahweh* has acquired several specific connotations. This holy name is the source of salvation for the people of God and the basis for the forgiveness of sins. As Psalm 79:9 puts it, "Help us, O God of our salvation, for the glory of your name; deliver us, and atone for our sins, for your name's sake!" This name is the only way by which people on earth may reach heaven. Even the temple in Jerusalem was only the residence of the name of the Lord, the God of Israel.

In the traditions of the people of Israel, the name of the Lord is revealed to the Israelites in the burning fire and in the "thunders and lightnings and a thick cloud." It is the source of salvation. Its power and holiness do not allow people to worship in any other way. One of the Ten Commandments says, "You shall not take the name of the Lord your God in vain." Religious Jews believe that humans are not allowed to mention the divine name. When they come across this name in reading the Hebrew scriptures, they substitute it with the word *Adonai* (meaning "my master") or *Ha-Shem* (meaning "the name"). Later, even the word *Adonai* could not be said but only *Ha-Shem*. In the liturgical traditions of the Israelites, only on the Day of Atonement each year did the high priest enter the holy of holies and place the sacrificial blood of the sacrifice on the mercy seat above the ark before he could call on the name of the Lord. In this way, he made "atonement for the Holy Place, because of the uncleanness of the people of Israel and because of their transgressions" (Lev 16:16).

From the theological traditions of the Old Testament, we can understand that at the fulfillment of prophecy God sent an angel to proclaim to humanity the meaning of the name Jesus. For human beings, who continue to sin and rebel, this is really good news. "The Lord, the Lord, a God merciful and gracious, slow to anger, and abounding in steadfast love and faithfulness" (Exod 34:6), sent his Son Jesus to save humanity. The name Jesus shows that God himself came and his name was revealed in his incarnate Son. The meaning of this name is "God saves." It is clearly revealed in Jesus' birth, mission, suffering, and resurrection. The divine nature inherent in this name is no longer concealed in darkness, no longer feared, but becomes an affable God who can be seen, heard, and touched. Through the name of Jesus, a close relationship between God and humanity was established: "I belong to you, and you belong to me."

Jesus is the name of a person from Nazareth, but it is also the name that is "above all names" (Phil 2:9). In pursuit of ultimate reality, the desire of the Israelites to establish an intimate and face-to-face relationship with God is encapsulated in this name. This name shows the combination of divinity and humanity; this name is light for people who sit in the shadow of death and darkness. This name stems from the will of God and was given by the mouth of the angel, and by this name humanity can come to God the Father. It is a person's name, but it encapsulates all that the people in the Old Testament prayed for when they called upon the Lord God. It can truly and universally redeem from sin; it is the only holy name that can bring salvation.

The identity of Christians originated from the recognition of the holy name of Jesus. They were all washed, sanctified, and justified in the name of the Lord Jesus (see 1 Cor 6:11). The fruitfulness in their lives is due to their constant petitions to God in the name of Jesus, because "Whatever you ask in my name, this I will do, that the Father may be glorified in the Son" (John 14:13). Calling on the holy name of Jesus has the nature of a sacrament; that is, in the visible voice of the lips the invisible reality of God and his actions are expressed. In the church's liturgy, the statement "in the name of Jesus" is usually attached at the end of ceremonial prayer. The name of Jesus is also the core of Christian prayer. To exclaim "Jesus" is to pray from the heart and to unite with him. Only the name Jesus, as this name implies, contains the presence of God. Whoever calls on Jesus' name welcomes the divine presence that was made possible by the Son who entered into human history at the incarnation.

In order to call on the holy name of Jesus, the universal church has developed a special prayer tradition, the Jesus Prayer. It includes several passages from the Gospels where people call upon the name of Jesus, including: "God, be merciful to me, a sinner!" (Luke 18:13); "Jesus, Son of David, have mercy on me!" (Luke 18:38); and "Lord, have mercy on us, Son of David!" (Matt 20:30). These instances have been summarized as: "Lord Jesus Christ, the Son of God, have mercy on me, a sinner." Or, to focus the mind, it was further simplified as: "Lord Jesus Christ, have mercy on me!"

This prayer centers on the name of Jesus and is a perfect summary of the Christian faith. The meaning of mercy is love. It bridges the bottomless abyss between the God of righteousness and depraved humanity through his love in Jesus, who is both God and man. The expression "have mercy" is both a helpless mourning and a hopeful exclamation. It truly confesses the reality of sin, but it also expresses the hope of a new day and calls for the forgiveness of sin. This is optimistic realism. It is a firm belief that although we are sinners, God, who lives in infinite glory, still accepts, renews, and transforms us. This prayer not only expresses our hope, it also gives us the assurance that we have already been accepted in Jesus. Therefore, the Jesus Prayer can be simplified to "my Jesus." It contains not only the call to repentance, but also the assurance of the forgiveness of sins and the restoration of God's children. Calling on the name of Jesus in prayer reveals the relationship of love between God and us and is the beginning of our redemption. It is also the beginning of the descending of his Spirit to us, strengthening and sanctifying us.

PRAYER

Almighty Lord God, you created all things through your holy name; you sustain all things, you protect all things, and you are gracious to all things. We pray that you will preserve us in our troubles through your holy name.

Merciful Lord, you revealed your name to your people; you are the eternal "I Am." May your faithfulness and mercy follow us all the days of our lives.

Compassionate Lord, you sent angels to reveal the name of the Savior to humanity, Jesus. Hear our prayer through Jesus and send your Spirit to us to heal us.

Lord Jesus, you are the king of heaven and earth. We ask you to hear our call in your holy name, and to bring us into your glorious kingdom.

Amen.

10

The Flight to Egypt

SCRIPTURE

"Now when they had departed, behold, an angel of the Lord appeared to Joseph in a dream and said, 'Rise, take the child and his mother, and flee to Egypt, and remain there until I tell you, for Herod is about to search for the child, to destroy him.' And he rose and took the child and his mother by night and departed to Egypt." (Matt 2:13–14)

"And Simeon blessed them and said to Mary his mother, 'Behold, this child is appointed for the fall and rising of many in Israel, and for a sign that is opposed, and a sword will pierce through your own soul also, so that thoughts from many hearts may be revealed.'" (Luke 2:35)

QUESTIONS

1. Upon becoming a man, how did Jesus face the sins and suffering of the world? How did his humanity endure suffering in the face of evil and darkness?

2. How did the flight to Egypt, which Jesus experienced shortly after his birth, herald his future mission? How does it foreshadow the suffering and death of Christ?

3. As a disciple, how do you participate in the mission of Jesus?

The Flight to Egypt

MEDITATION

In the overall atmosphere of the joy, peace, and praise of the first Christmas, these passages are very instructive. In church tradition, they respectively relate to the prophecy of Jesus' suffering and death and the flight to Egypt, which constitute two of the seven pains Mary experienced. The two passages describing events shortly after Jesus' birth point to the pain and death that Jesus would endure in the world. In a quiet and subtle way, they bring the two events of Jesus' coming into the world and leaving the world closely together, the important events of life and death. Such a juxtaposition allows people to feel Lent's suffering and darkness while they celebrated the joy and light of Advent.

These two passages raise several questions for our meditation. When the Word became flesh, how did he face the sins and suffering of the world? To suffer with the people of the world, how did he hide his divinity? In the face of evil and darkness, how did his humanity endure suffering?

Like other passages in the Gospels' testimony of Jesus' birth, the passage of the flight to Egypt is also full of Old Testament allusions. Only in light of God's revelation in the Old Testament can we understand these passages accurately and deeply. There are two passages in the Old Testament that we need to consider. The first passage is Exodus 1:15—2:10:

> Then the king of Egypt said to the Hebrew midwives . . . "When you serve as midwife to the Hebrew women and see them on the birthstool, if it is a son, you shall kill him, but if it is a daughter, she shall live." . . . Now a man from the house of Levi went and took as his wife a Levite woman. The woman conceived and bore a son, and when she saw that he was a fine child, she hid him three months. When she could hide him no longer, she took for him a basket made of bulrushes and daubed it with bitumen and pitch. She put the child in it and placed it among the reeds by the river bank. . . . When the child grew older, she brought him to Pharaoh's daughter, and he became her son. She named him Moses, "Because," she said, "I drew him out of the water."

The second passage is Jeremiah 31:15:

> Thus says the Lord: "A voice is heard in Ramah, lamentation and bitter weeping. Rachel is weeping for her children; she refuses to be comforted for her children, because they are no more."

Both Old Testament passages describe the demise of Israel in history. The former relates to the time when the Israelites were living in Egypt and Pharaoh intended to exterminate them and kill all Israelite boys. In this tragedy of infanticide, Moses survived and eventually led the Israelites out of Egypt. The latter passage relates to the time of the prophet Jeremiah. At that time, the Assyrian Empire had already devastated the northern kingdom. Israel had already gone into exile and the prophet Jeremiah mourned for the northern kingdom. According to Genesis, Rachel was Joseph's mother and Joseph was the ancestor of the two core tribes in the north: Manasseh and Ephraim. Therefore, Joseph represented the entire northern kingdom of Israel. Therefore, the image of Rachel crying for her children denotes the demise of the northern kingdom of Israel.

Thus, shortly after Jesus' birth, Joseph and Mary had to take Jesus and flee to Egypt. Herod was killing all the boys in Bethlehem and all its surrounding territory, just as Pharaoh tried to kill all the Israelite boys, and just as the Assyrian Empire destroyed the northern kingdom. Later, Jesus was crucified on a cross, which was the main reason why the Word became flesh and entered the world. God's holy Son entered a world full of sin, violence, and murder. The Word becoming flesh brought hope and light to people sitting in the darkness of death, but it also placed Jesus in a dangerous situation. Because of the wickedness of the human heart, humans constantly create various idols to make themselves the masters of others and of the world. Because of the constant temptations of the devil, this world is always full of cruelty and tyranny. As it says in Romans 3:13–16, "Their throat is an open grave; they use their tongues to deceive. The venom of asps is under their lips. Their mouth is full of curses and bitterness. Their mouth is full of curses and bitterness, in their paths are ruin and misery."

The suffering caused by sin in the world is real. The divine child, who was both divine and human, did not use his divinity to drive away suffering. On the contrary, he suffered and experienced suffering through his true humanity. Jesus became a refugee with Mary and Joseph. Between Israel and Egypt, there is a long historical tradition of flight. In a time of great famine, Jacob and his sons who lived in Canaan fled to Egypt; to avoid Pharaoh's pursuit, Moses fled into Midian; Jeroboam fled Egypt to escape the persecution of Solomon. Apart from the holy family, there were probably many others who fled to Egypt to avoid Herod's massacre. Jesus and the holy family became part of the refugees with no guarantee of safety or food. Among the refugees, the Son is among those who suffered in humble

The Flight to Egypt

circumstances. Later, when Jesus was teaching, there was a question from one of the disciples: "'Lord, when did we see you hungry and feed you, or thirsty and give you drink? And when did we see you a stranger and welcome you, or naked and clothe you? And when did we see you sick or in prison and visit you?' And the King will answer them, 'Truly, I say to you, as you did it to one of the least of these my brothers, you did it to me'" (Matt 25:37–40). Jesus also fled to Egypt, reminding us to see the reflection of the Son in the face of refugees and to see Christ in those who live on the margins.

Shortly after Jesus was born, his family was warned, and they fled to Egypt. Herod began to kill all who were under two years of age around Bethlehem. Without referring to other massacres, this event allows us to see the cruelty and suffering that stem from sin. However, the Son of God did not use magic or witchcraft to expel sin and suffering, but personally used his human nature to experience and endure the suffering of the world. Just as when the Israelites were oppressed by the Egyptians, the Lord said to Moses, "I have surely seen the affliction of my people who are in Egypt and have heard their cry because of their taskmasters. I know their sufferings, and I have come down to deliver them out of the hand of the Egyptians and to bring them up out of that land to a good and broad land, a land flowing with milk and honey" (Exod 3:7–8). The newly born Jesus not only saw, heard, and knew, but experienced for himself all the physical and mental suffering of the world. More particularly, in the end he gave his life as a sacrifice on the cross to bear the pain of death on behalf of humanity.

This flight, which Jesus experienced shortly after his birth, is typological of his struggle against the dark world of human suffering and sin. In the glory and joy of the incarnation, we perceive the appearance of this dark world, and after Jesus began his ministry this dark power grew stronger and stronger until he was crucified for the sins of the world. "Now from the sixth hour there was darkness over all the land until the ninth hour" (Matt 27:45). What is the source of this dark power? It originated from the Satan's first temptation, but also from the weakness of human nature, which yielded to the temptation. The original sin of Adam drove people to become slaves of the devil, who had the power of death. Generations of people have again and again aggravated this situation with their own sins and have caused the world to fall into the predicament of enslaving sin. Jesus and the holy family had to flee to Egypt, reflecting the reality that "the whole world lies in the power of the evil one" (1 John 5:19). It also reminds all who are determined to follow Christ that life is a struggle. The entire history of humanity, from the moment of creation, has been a tough battle against the forces of darkness. When people live in this battlefield, they must continue to fight. In this war, we need to pray and to rely on the grace of God, always remembering to "have the mind of the heart of Christ" (Phil 2:5) and drawing on the power of freedom and wisdom from the Holy Spirit.

Jesus fled to Egypt shortly after his birth. The prediction in the temple regarding Mary that "a sword will pierce through your own soul" shows that this Savior who entered the world would redeem humanity in a paradoxical way. He would use suffering, even death, to earn eternal life for humanity. His suffering was not imaginary. With Herod's massacre of infants, Jesus also had to become a refugee with others. Therefore, we should not imagine that there will be a burst of divine power to expel misery. To suffer like a human being was the way in which Jesus responded to suffering.

This leads us to meditate on the paradoxes of life. Light is to expel the darkness, and life is to redeem death. It suggests the following kind of lifestyle for Christians: children of God, leave paradise, go down into the world! Go to toil in the world, go to serve the world, go to be spurned and be crucified for the sake of the world! Life is given in order to be taken; the bread of eternal life descends in order to suffer hunger (Matt 21:18); the true way came down in order to be weary along the road (John 4:6); the living fountain sprang up in order to feel thirst (John 19:28). But, do you refuse to suffer?

PRAYER

Jesus, you are the Son of the living God; you are light from light. We cry to you, Lord, come and lead us into the light!

You are the Word of eternal life. The world was created by you, and you came to your own place, yet it did not receive you. You bore the suffering and through your blood shed on the cross you redeemed us. We pray that you now come and fill us. Give us courage and strength to withstand persecution and courage to fight.

Jesus, you are the eternal light. We now beseech you to arouse our faith from the darkness. Let us be saturated with your glory. According to your word, help us to treat people with goodness and disperse the darkness of the world.

Lord, come to us. Starting from our hearts, create a new world and let peace and justice flourish among humanity.

Amen!

11

My Father's Business

SCRIPTURE

"And He said to them, 'Why did you seek Me? Did you not know that I must be about My Father's business?'" (Luke 2:49 NKJ)

"And because you are sons, God has sent the Spirit of his Son into our hearts, crying, 'Abba! Father!'" (Gal 4:6)

QUESTIONS

1. How was Jesus occupied with his "Father's business" during his lifetime?
2. Why does the birth of Jesus permit us also to call upon God as "Abba Father"?
3. What does calling God "Father" imply about the nature of the Christian life? What responsibilities come with calling God "Father"?

MEDITATION

In the narrative of Luke's gospel, at the age of twelve, according to Jewish tradition, Jesus went to Jerusalem to join the Passover celebration. After Passover, he stayed behind in the temple to study the Scriptures and did not return home with Joseph and Mary. When Mary found Jesus, she reprimanded him for not returning with them to Nazareth. Jesus then referred to his holy identity: "Why did you seek me? Did you not know that I must be about my Father's business?" (Luke 2:49). This is the first time that Jesus calls God "Father" in the Gospels; the use of the term clarified the close relationship between Jesus and God. At the same time, Jesus also pointed out that he should be busy with his "Father's business"; that is, he was at one with the Father in love and will.

Jesus was the Word who became flesh. He obtained complete humanity from Mary's womb. His human nature was real, just like yours and mine. He had both a body as well as a soul. Therefore, he also experienced joy, anger, grief, and joy like us. He had human-like freedom of will, which was always subservient to the Father's will to accomplish everything in the plan of salvation. Jesus' words that he must be about his "Father's business" indicate that Jesus' human will freely obeyed the will of God Almighty.

Another perfect example of Jesus willingly and freely submitting his human will to the divine will is his prayer in Gethsemane in the night before the crucifixion. As revealed by the Hebrew connotation of Gethsemane (which means "oil press"), Gethsemane was the place where Jesus was "crushed" for the sake of humanity. In the events that took place at Gethsemane and Golgotha, Jesus completely subjected his will to the will of the Father, which was that he drink the cup of suffering to save the world. So, Jesus prayed, "Father, if you are willing, remove this cup from me. Nevertheless, not my will, but yours, be done" (Luke 22:42). Such complete obedience was paradoxically implied in Jesus' opening address to God as "Father." The intimacy of the Father and Son shows both that Jesus had complete freedom and that he was willing to do the Father's will. The will of the Father and the will of the Son are in complete harmony.

"Abba, Father," a daily family expression, reveals the inner mystery of the Holy Trinity. The Father is in the Son, the Son is in the Father, and the love between them is communicated by the third person, the Holy Spirit. This sacred mystery was not only revealed in the teachings of Jesus, but also through his condescension and through the cross, accomplishing his "Father's business." He veiled his divine sonship and emptied himself in order that a multitude of people may become the children of God. Because of his crucifixion and resurrection, every believer may now cry out to the highest God as "Abba, Father," which is the core of the gospel Jesus brought to humanity.

People have coined many theological terms to express the benefits of salvation people receive from God, but the most common and highest expression is the whisper "Abba, Father." The apostle Paul forthrightly declared that believers could use this expression because the triune God has come to meet with us in our hearts. Those who can cry "Abba, Father" are those to whom the triune God has revealed himself. "God has sent the Spirit of his Son into our hearts, crying, 'Abba! Father!'" (Gal 4:6). It is the voice of the Holy Spirit that cries out in our hearts; it does not come from our own efforts. Secondly, this Holy Spirit is the Spirit of his Son, who alone may cry out "Abba." Finally, the Son proceeds from the supreme God; he was destined before the creation of the universe to accomplish his will in the plan of salvation by means of the Father-Son relationship.

Because the persons of the Holy Trinity, in its *perichrosis*, moved people's hearts, people can cry "Abba, Father" in Christ, and thus confirm their identity as God's children. This reminds us of two important moments in the life of Jesus: his baptism and his transfiguration. In these two events, there was a voice from heaven saying, "This is my beloved Son, with whom I am well pleased" (Matt 3:17; 17:5). The confirmation of the identity of Jesus as "beloved Son" is also completely the work of the Holy Trinity. In the baptism of Jesus, the Holy Spirit took the form of a dove, descended from heaven, and rested upon him. In Jesus' transfiguration, the "bright cloud" represented the presence of the Holy Spirit. On these two occasions where Jesus was identified as the "beloved Son," the persons of the Holy Trinity were present together: the Father was represented by the voice, the Son took on the form of a human, and the Holy Spirit was represented by the cloud or the dove. Since then, every Christian's status as a beloved child is confirmed in every invisible human heart when he or she cries, "Abba, Father." But what remains unchanged is that the Father, the Son, and the Holy Spirit all participate in our yearning for God as his children.

It is an extremely great honor to call the Creator of heaven and earth "Father." When Moses first heard God's call, "Moses! Moses!" he also heard the command, "Do not come near" (Exod 3:5). People would not dare to imagine that there could be a close father-son relationship with the Creator, nor can the angels understand it. But, by faith in Jesus, through the leading of the Spirit, we may cry out to God as "Abba, Father." As Tertullian said, "The name 'Father God' has never been revealed to anyone before. When Moses asked God: "What is your name?," he heard another name. The name "Father" was revealed in the "Son" because it was in the Son that it contained the new name of God—Father.[1] Without the incarnation of the Son, how could miserable humanity be qualified to call God "Father"? The birth of the Son of God provided for our reconciliation to God and to be accepted as the children of God. Even in the words of Cyril of Jerusalem (313–386 CE), we not only became children of God, but also Christ in the plural. He said, "Indeed, the God who has destined us to be accepted as his children, has molded us into the body of Christ. Thus, you, the sharers in Christ, may aptly be called 'Christs.'"[2]

By means of the Son becoming one of us, we may call God "Father," which, in another more comprehensive dimension, realizes the deep desire for the ideal life in Chinese culture. During the Northern Song Dynasty, Zhang Zai (1020–1077) once gave a refined summary of this ideal life. He believed that heaven and earth were his parents and that he was like a weak child in the world. The space of heaven and earth was his body and the power that governs the universe was in his nature. All people were his brothers and sisters born of the same parents; everything in heaven and earth was also part of his own substance.[3] In the Chinese cultural tradition, heaven (Qian, 乾) and earth (Kun, 坤) are the ultimate reality. Only those who regard heaven and earth as their parents are in touch with reality and can establish a relationship with all human beings as their fellow brothers and friends.

The Christian faith believes that through the coming of the Son people can reach such ideals of life at a deeper level. The Holy Trinity was originally a family of love, with father-like and child-like characteristics, with a constant stream of love flowing between the persons (through the Holy Spirit). Through the birth of the Son, as the ultimate reality of the universe, the love of the Holy Trinity spilled into the world, and every believer may now call God "Father." We are born into the loving relationship of the Holy Trinity; our bodies have become the temple of the Holy Spirit; our will is united in the relationship of love in the Holy Trinity. Every believer may now call God "Father" as a child; all believers through love as brothers and sisters constitute the family of God—the church. Everything in the universe

---

1. Tertullian, *On Prayer*, 682.
2. See Catholic Church, *Catechism of Catholic Church*, no. 2782.
3. As Zhang Zai said: "We may call Heaven our father and Earth our mother, and we are their children in between, although we are small. Therefore, I am part of reality as my body is filled with the essence of heaven and earth, the principle of heaven and earth is in our nature. Therefore, we should regard all people as our brothers and all things as equal." Zhang Zai, *Words on the West Wall*, 62.

is also connected to the loving fellowship of the Creator through the tangible elements of the sacraments, which express invisible grace.

Therefore, the address "Father" is the first sound that opens all our prayers. The first statement of the Lord's Prayer is: "Our Father, who is in heaven." Firstly, this is the sound of worship and praise to the Father. It shows that we are children who want to enter heaven (Matt 18:3). We are born again in his Son and anointed in the Holy Spirit and so become God's children. This privilege requires us to purify our hearts humbly and to join the family of the Holy Trinity with the mind of a child just like the relationship between children and their parents. We shall be filled with a mood of simplicity and warmth, honesty and happiness, humility and boldness, full of love. In this kind of trust and love, we may enter the depths of the love of God, melt our soul in the fire of love, and integrate our lives into the life of the Holy Trinity. In this way, calling God "Father" leads to the purification of our own lives. In addition, a voice that calls out "Father" does not monopolize the Father's love but shares it with others.

Secondly, the cry "Father" expresses our desire to follow and learn from Jesus. We are sinners, but we become righteous through the righteousness of God's only begotten Son. Christ is the only begotten Son of God. We are all created by God. We are accepted as his children in Christ; that is, it is only through grace that we may pray, "Our Father." Therefore, when we call God "Father," we must continue to follow and learn from Jesus in grace, to become more and more like him in our words and deeds, so that we can live lives that are commensurate with the identity of the children of God. The key to learning from Jesus is to imitate his humility as a child and to subdue our will to God's will, and to say, "I must be about my Father's business," or as he prayed in Gethsemane, "Not my will, but yours be done."

Finally, the cry "Father" reminds us to remember God's other children. We are not the only children of God. We are not the "only begotten Son," but are adopted children. Because we have been joined with others to God's only begotten Son, the Lord's Prayer emphasizes "our" Father. Therefore, when we pray to God as "Father," we are not the only ones praying. It is our worship of the Holy Father together with the Son and the Holy Spirit. It is also our prayer to the Father in heaven together with the universal church. All who believe in Jesus as the only begotten Son and who have been born again through the Spirit are God's children. When people pray the Lord's Prayer and pray in the name of Jesus to "our Father," it is through the compulsion of God's love, that they move away from self-centeredness and join the celestial worship of the heavenly celebration.

PRAYER

Lord Jesus, incarnate Son of God, you are the future that has come. We pray to you, Lord, come to us now!

Lord, begotten Son of the Father before the creation of the world, you descended and became a human being to be our elder brother. Let us through you become sons and daughters of the heavenly Father. Be gracious to us that we may be worthy of the title "children of God."

Lord, you were obedient to the Father's will in all your life and willingly embraced God's plan of salvation. Fill us with your Holy Spirit so that we may continually know the will of God and live in obedience and in the love of God.

Holy Lord, as the firstborn of God, lead us all and all things into the worship of God the Father. Continually remind us to lay aside our selfishness and to desire that all things in the world come into the embrace of the Father.

Amen.

12

Prepare the Way of the Lord, Make His Paths Straight

SCRIPTURE

"The voice of one crying in the wilderness: 'Prepare the way of the Lord, make his paths straight.'" (Mark 1:3)

"From that time Jesus began to preach, saying, 'Repent, for the kingdom of heaven is at hand.'" (Matt 4:17)

QUESTIONS

1. How can we "make his paths straight"? How can we "prepare the way of the Lord"? Where are the paths of the Lord?

2. Advent commemorates the coming of the Lord Jesus at Christmas. How should we prepare our hearts now for the coming of the Lord?

3. Why is repentance a continual requirement for Christians? What is the significance of repentance for Christian growth? How can we use repentance to "prepare the way of the Lord" and "make his paths straight"?

MEDITATION

After three decades of growing up with his parents, Jesus was about to present his Word to the world. At this time, there appeared a voice heralding the coming of Christ: "Prepare the way of the Lord, make his paths straight." These were the words of John the Baptist. But this voice from the mouth of the last prophet before Christ was the voice of God's Holy Word. It was pointing to the Holy Word that was about to enter the world in physical form.

This text is particularly suitable for meditating on Christmas, because it tells us how to prepare for the coming of the Lord. How can we "make his paths straight"? How can we "prepare the way of the Lord"? Where are paths of the Lord and the way of the Lord?

In the four Gospels, there is no mention of an example in which Jesus asked his disciples to smooth out a road to welcome him. What kind of path would the Lord, who could walk on water, be unable to walk? Obviously, the "way" and "paths" here do not refer to actual physical roads. They refer to our thoughts, words, and behavior. Our hearts and minds are the places where the word of the Lord can penetrate. Our words and deeds are the way the Lord walks in our lives. Our body, mind, and will are the way and paths in which we interact with the Lord. In our thoughts, words, and actions, we are moving toward the Lord. The Lord is also moving toward us in our thoughts, words, and actions. The activities of our hearts, minds, and lives are the way we interact with the Lord. This is the way we have to prepare, and it is also the path that we must straighten out.

How can we "prepare the way of the Lord" and "make his paths straight"? Before John cited the prophet's Isaiah cry, he first exclaimed, "Repent, for the kingdom of heaven is at hand" (Matt 3:2). This command is an explanation for how one should "prepare the way of the Lord." "Repent" was also the first command that came when Jesus began to preach the gospel (Matt 4:17). Indeed, repentance is the best way for us to prepare the way of the Lord and to straighten his paths.

What is repentance? The first element of repentance is *sincerity*, that is, facing yourself in a fearless spirit of self-reflection. Any of our intentions is a movement of our heart, and any moving of the heart would produce an intention. People's intentions are unpredictable, changeable, fleeting, and difficult to comprehend. Good people, through obeying God's laws, observe the principles of life; maintain good relationships between those in high positions and low positions, between the old and the young, between husbands and wives, and between brothers and the friends; and obey all the institutions of human civilization. As the ideal person, the "gentleman" (or "sage"), achieves his life goal in the human order. The gentleman always endeavors to honor God and to benefit people. However, those who are not good pursue their own selfish desires and are led by their lusts. They worship various forms of creation as idols. Sincerity is the true face of the self. The author of Hebrews challenges his readers in this way: "Let us draw near with a true heart in full assurance of faith, with our hearts sprinkled clean from an evil conscience and our bodies washed with pure water" (Heb 10:22).

The second element of repentance is *uprightness of heart* or *righteousness*, which is the transformation of the mind. The mind is the source of ideas, and it is also the motivating force of good or evil desires. The heart contains all kinds of good ends. Kindness, righteousness, propriety, and wisdom all stem from the heart, but it is also tempted by sensual things and often fashions created things into idols, which then become the masters of life. Uprightness of heart or righteousness is the transformation of the mind. By being no longer obsessed with using various created things as idols, it turns to the God who has revealed his commandments in the Bible. Therefore, the Old Testament prophets always called Israel to repentance with the words "turn around" as the core of the call. In fact, repentance includes two aspects, that of "remorse" and that of "perseverance" (resistance, fortitude, serenity). The former spurs us on to practice kindness, righteousness, propriety, and wisdom, and the latter enables us to resist sensuality and impropriety (动其仁义礼智之心，忍其声色臭味之性).[1] It enables people to correctly distinguish between the important matters of life, between causes and effects, as well as to cultivate the inner qualities of righteousness and to control the excesses of sensual desires. One should not suffocate love because of selfish desires. One should not smother benevolence because of greed. One should not lose something big to gain something small, nor should one neglect a principle for the sake of pursuing a certain end.

When Jesus entered Jerusalem in the last week of his life, he came to the temple of God and saw that it was full of cattle, sheep, and pigeons with money changers doing business. He took some ropes and made a whip and proceeded to drive out the animals and to turn over the tables of the money changers, and said, "Take these things away; do not make my Father's house

---

1. Zhu Xi, *Zhu Xi's Conversations*, vol. 59.

a house of trade" (John 2:16). This action by Jesus demonstrates the meaning of heartfelt sincerity. Our heart is the temple of God, but it is often occupied by various desires. The work of sincerity is to remove all evil desires and evil thoughts, to keep the heart and mind clean, and to welcome the coming of the Lord.

The third element of repentance is being renewed day by day. Repentance is the breathing of our hearts in the Holy Spirit. Repentance causes us to remove impurities of all kinds and enables us to obtain new motivation and power from the Holy Spirit in prayer. Repentance puts our hearts in a state of humility and opens a door in our hearts so that the breath of the Holy Spirit can enter us. Repentance is the breath of life. We have to breath out our foul air and inhale the pure air of God's Spirit. In this way, our hearts will be reconciled with the Tao (the Way), be renewed, and receive power for life. Repentance is not a one-off event; it is the way our spiritual life grows and renews day by day. At the same time, repentance does not allow us to focus on the uncleanness and defilement in the depths of our hearts. Instead, it redirects our attention to God to rejoice in sharing our lives with the Holy Trinity.

In Chinese, "repentance" is a compound word consisting of the two ideas of penitence and change; penitence is its starting point while change is its end. A person who regards his life as a journey and welcomes the Lord's coming will experience remorse, but remorse will not remain in the heart for long. Keeping turbidity in one's chest is not conducive to the renewal of life. Repentance begins with humility, contrition, tears, and confession, but its purpose is to bear the fruits of a new life: forgiveness, peace, and unity. The essence of repentance has to do with change; as Zhu Xi (1130–1200) said, there will be no regrets if one has changed.[2] Change involves regret, but it will also transform and enhance regret. Making change the center of repentance will bear the fruits of love, forgiveness, and peace in life.

The words of John the Baptist "prepare the way of the Lord, make his paths straight" remind us during the season of Christmas that we not only celebrate during Christmas, but we also need to learn a lesson. We need to let the one we celebrate come and change us.

When Christ comes, we need to open the doors of our heart through repentance. We need to prepare the way of the Lord in our hearts. In this way, Christ can enter our hearts along the paths of our lives. Christ will come to us and be born in our hearts. We may then also offer the gifts of

---

2. Zhu Xi, *Zhu Xi's Conversations*, vol. 29.

the virtues of our life to this newborn king. We do not offer myrrh, but we offer repentance; we do not offer frankincense, but we offer prayers; we do not offer gold, but we offer love. Only a pure heart can celebrate a pure Christmas.

PRAYER

Lord Jesus, we look forward to your coming. Open the kingdom of God for us on the earth.

Lord God, send your Holy Spirit into our hearts. Renew our minds to prepare the way for the coming of your Holy Son.

Lord God, we welcome the coming of your Holy Son. Establish your kingdom on the earth and grant us grace to bear the fruit of repentance.

Lord God, subdue our pride, rectify our shortcomings, and transform the harshness in our hearts into a smooth path.

Lord Jesus, dismantle the barriers of division and hatred among people, and build a harmonious path for all.

Amen.

13

The Last Adam

SCRIPTURE

"Jesus, when he began his ministry, was about thirty years of age, being the son (as was supposed) of Joseph, the son of Heli, . . . the son of Enos, the son of Seth, the son of Adam, the son of God." (Luke 3:23, 38)

"Thus it is written, 'The first man Adam became a living being; the last Adam became a life-giving spirit.' . . . The first man was from the earth, a man of dust; the second man is from heaven." (1 Cor 15:45, 47)

QUESTIONS

1. Why was Adam called "the son of God"? What does this title indicate about his spiritual identity?
2. What is the significance in the plan of creation of Jesus being the "last Adam"?
3. How did the birth of the last Adam, Jesus, restore the image and mission of the first Adam?

MEDITATION:

After describing Jesus' birth, Luke recorded Jesus' genealogy. He traced the source of the genealogy through Abraham, all the way back to Adam, referring to Adam as "the son of God." What revelation did Luke intended to give us about Jesus in the genealogy? Why was Christ born under Adam? What is the significance of calling Jesus "the last Adam" or "the second man" in terms of God's creation plan (see 1 Cor 15: 45)? How can we be the descendants of Adam and be born again through the Holy Spirit into the "last Adam"? How did the birth of the "second man" restore the mission of the "first man" to us?

Genesis opens with the magnificent story of creation. In this story, the creation of Adam takes up the most space. The description of Adam's creation in Genesis 2:5–8 is concrete and vivid. Compared with it, the definition of human nature in Genesis 1:26–28 is abstract and broad. But they echo each other and give people a comprehensive understanding of the nature and mission of original humanity.

These two passages explain the question "Who was Adam?" and also constitute the Bible's answer to the question "What is man?" Adam had two basic identities: one is the image of God; the other is as a "living being." The most intuitive and basic meaning of the word "image" relates to a reflection or a likeness. In other words, humans may reflect or be a likeness of the glory of God. In simple terms, in all of creation, Adam was most like God. Then, what temperament of the human reflects the glory of God? What aspect of human nature is most like God?

According to the first chapter of Genesis, God is the creator of the world, and his divinity is demonstrated in his freedom to create the world. He did not create the world out of any necessity. His creation was not constrained by any conditions. Creation was made out of nothing and God's will was the only reason for the creation of the world. Man was created on the last day of creation, reflecting the free nature of God. Adam had complete freedom, self-reflection, rational thinking, and responsibility. His freedom was absolutely true, and it included the freedom to rebel against God's command. In the garden of Eden, in his freedom Adam could even refuse to realize his moral and spiritual power and refuse to follow and listen to God. In abstract terms, man is the image of God; from the specific human aspect, man can engage with God because God breathes his breath into the nostrils of man. Adam was a "living soul." Therefore, humans may hear God, perceive God, and respond to God in their spirit or soul.

The Last Adam

This is the meaning of the image of Adam that we see in our original creation. Among all the creatures, humans enjoy the highest privilege; in the human, the material world and the spiritual world converge. The human also possesses the ability of two dimensions. In the horizontal dimension, people can recognize themselves, own themselves, decide for themselves, freely offer themselves, communicate with others, and govern others as a subject; in the vertical dimension, people can enter into a covenant with the Creator, and in the deepest part of their being respond to God with faith and love. Therefore, Adam was called "the son of God" in Luke.

Adam was the first person of human genealogy and his spouse, Eve, was made of one of his ribs. All people of different races and cultures are his descendants. Through Adam and Eve, God created the entire human race on the earth. In Adam's body, according to biblical revelation, the whole family of the world and the ideal human being was represented. Humanity began in Adam; from him all humans descended. He represents the ideal human being in Christianity. The so-called one source of human beings refers not only to God, the creator, but also to the first person, Adam (Acts 17:26). As a result, human beings have the same nature and are composed of body and soul. Humanity also has the same living mission and goal as Adam. Human beings live in the same place, on the planet earth, and everyone has the right to share in the natural resources of the earth. Since everyone is born of Adam, everyone in the world is also ethically responsible for each other's well-being in mutual love. This is the foundation of Christianity's concept of the brotherhood of human beings. According to Genesis 1 and 2, there is no room for the concept of barbarian. People born in all kinds of cultures and ethnic groups are brothers and sisters in Adam.

On an individual level, the human being is a free subject. On a social level, the human being is part of a group. These are the two basic connotations of God's creation of Adam as the ancestor of humanity. However, because Adam used his freedom in the wrong way and violated God's command, he was expelled from paradise and separated from God. Since then, humanity has become a slave to sin and death and has lost its freedom in God. The descendants of Adam have also become enemies. Gender politics has led to a dispute between women and men in terms of power struggles. Brothers fell into hatred of one another just as Cain murdered Abel. Fighting between ethnic groups arose; one group of people tried to become the masters over another group of people. After the tower of Babel, the confusion of languages further split the unity of humanity apart. So today people are scattered across the earth according to blood, language, and culture.

However, the original plan of God at creation was not lost. The birth of Jesus was to restore the original mission that God gave to humanity when Adam was created. In this sense, Jesus is the "second Adam." This is also the reason why Luke traced Jesus' genealogy all the way back to Adam and referred to Adam as "the son of God."

Why did Jesus, born in the Roman era, recover the image that Adam had at the beginning of creation? The incarnation of Jesus was able to restore Adam from before the coming of sin. In fact, Christ participated in the creation of the original Adam. As Paul said, "The first man Adam became a living being; the last Adam became a life-giving spirit" (1 Cor 15:45). Christ was the Word of God, and when the Creator first created Adam, Jesus participated in that creation. Christ created Adam, who was the "image of the firstborn" (Col 1:15), and he received his soul from Christ and became a living being. Christ carved his own image into Adam. The reason why Christ was born to the descendants of Adam was to restore God's image in humanity. Christ took on the image of Adam to restore the image of Christ in Adam at creation.

How did Christ restore Adam's original image? By becoming a man, Jesus became the son of Adam. He opened up a new possibility for fallen humanity: humanity, which was created in God's image, could be enlightened by the glory of God and be recreated to reflect the glory of God. Christ fully subordinated his human will to God's will to abolish the sting and strength of the devil in holding and destroying life. He did this through his divine-human communion in the loving obedience of Gethsemane and the cross. Just as the first Adam was led astray by the devil because of disobedience, the last Adam has shown the power of God and the original image of humanity in his loving obedience to God. This is what Paul said: "For as by the one man's disobedience the many were made sinners, so by the one man's obedience the many will be made righteous. Now the law came in to increase the trespass, but where sin increased, grace abounded all the more so that, as sin reigned in death, grace also might reign through righteousness leading to eternal life through Jesus Christ our Lord" (Rom 5:19–21). The victory achieved by Jesus on the cross and the empty tomb become the source of joy and hope for all people. Those who accept Christ as the Lord of life not only are free from the bondage of death, and reverse the power of sin, but also share in the blessing originally enjoyed by Adam.

Christ entered the history of humanity as a descendant of Adam in order to enable humanity to be restored into the unity it had in Adam. As the descendants of the first Adam, we are scattered over the earth to belong to different nations, languages, and cultures. So too in Christ we will be regathered into one people of God. Through the incarnation of Christ, God became our Father and the church our mother. Through the rebirth by the "water and the Spirit" (John 3:5), we can call Jesus our elder brother and be accepted as "the children of God." This is what Paul said in Galatians 3:27–28: "For as many of you as were baptized into Christ have put on Christ. There is neither Jew nor Greek, there is neither slave nor free, there is no male and female, for you are all one in Christ Jesus." n Christ, the ideal of the brotherhood of all people existing at the time of the original Adam may be attained because that is the hope and mission of the church as the body of Christ.

Christ was born as a descendant of Adam, not only to restore the original Adam in us, but also to give us a greater glory than Adam. The Word became flesh and lived in the world, showing us what it means to be a saint. He declared to us Eight Blessings and guided us in the practice of virtue to walk in faith leading to heaven. He gave us the "new commandment." demanding that his disciples become a community of love. "You must love one another, as I have loved you" (John 15:12). As the ceremonial high priest, he integrated the ceremonial activities of the earth into the heavenly worship of God, and he consecrated by his Holy Spirit the bread and wine to represent his body and blood, enabling believers to become one with him and to live in harmony with each other.

The Word became flesh, and the Son entered the world according to the genealogy of Adam. The incarnation enabled humanity to communicate with the Word (communion) and to be united with the Word (union) in the highest realm of life. This allows us to share in God's nature; as Irenaeus puts it, "The Word became a man, and the reason why the Son of God became the Son of Man, is to bring people into harmony with the Word and to become the children of God."

PRAYER

Lord Jesus, Adam was made by you and lived by you. You created life not for it to perish. You searched for Adam and released him from pain and suffering.

Lord, you are not far away from us. We pray that you show yourself to those who seek for you.

Lord, you are the wealth of the poor, the comfort of the mourners; you set slaves free and let the afflicted ones rejoice.

Lord, you became one of us to open a new path for us to return to paradise. Restore to us the eternal life that was lost by Adam.

Amen.

PART III

Christ Is Born into Us

14

The Poor

SCRIPTURE

"Blessed are you who are poor, for yours is the kingdom of God." (Luke 6:20)

"Blessed are the poor in spirit, for theirs is the kingdom of heaven." (Matt 5:3)

"For you know the grace of our Lord Jesus Christ, that though he was rich, yet for your sake he became poor, so that you by his poverty might become rich." (2 Cor 8:9)

QUESTIONS

1. Why should the new life in Christ begin by meditating on the Beatitudes?
2. What kind of life do the Beatitudes reveal to us?
3. What are the practical and spiritual implications of "poverty"? How do Christians learn the poverty of Jesus?
4. How do we carry out our responsibilities to God, to others, and to nature in living the "poor" life?

MEDITATION

In meditating on Christmas, we may focus our thoughts on the eight Beatitudes in the Gospels. Why meditate on the Beatitudes during Christmas? In the Gospels of Matthew and Luke, the Beatitudes are announced at the beginning of Jesus' Sermon on the Mount. When Jesus first began to preach to the people, he announced the Beatitudes. The Beatitudes are the blessings of Jesus on eight categories of people. They are praises for the eight virtues of human life. But further, the Beatitudes also describe what Jesus said about himself. The Beatitudes are an explanation of his mission to the world and in his own life he practiced the virtues of the eight blessings. Our celebration of Christmas today is not only to commemorate the Christmas event that took place in Israel more than two thousand years ago, but also to allow Christ to be born into our lives. In this sense, when we meditate on Christmas, we also contemplate the Beatitudes. We want to live our lives according to the Beatitudes. In this way, by imitating Christ we allow the life of Christ to be born in us.

In a deeper sense, the Beatitudes are based on the Ten Commandments, which Moses received at Sinai. The Ten Commandments are the revelation that Moses received from God. But they are also the axioms of human society and an indispensable ethical code for an orderly civilization. It is interesting to note that the Ten Commandments conclude with "do not covet." This is a special commandment since it does not prohibit any external action, but it brings the commandment into the realm of the mind and thoughts. It can be said that the tenth commandment is a summary of the previous nine commandments; it sets up a goal that needs continuous improvement: purify your hearts. It is an endless task, and it is a goal that cannot be measured by external standards. It is intended to remind us that all the commandments are directed to people's hearts.

In the same way, we may note that the Beatitudes of Jesus in the Gospel of Matthew are an echo of the Ten Commandments of Moses in the book of Exodus. Firstly, Jesus "went up on the mountain" (Matt 5:1) to declare several commands, showing that he is a new Moses who issues new commandments on the mountain. Secondly, the Ten Commandments act as a summary of the Old Testament law given at Sinai. Therefore, the Beatitudes are also a summary of the new law of Jesus and the charter of the kingdom of heaven. In addition, strictly speaking, the blessings of Matthew 5 are not eight in number but ten, since they also include Matthew 5:11, "Blessed are you when others revile you and persecute you and utter all kinds of evil against you falsely on my account," and Matthew 5:12, "Rejoice and be glad, for your reward is great in heaven, for so they persecuted the prophets who were before you." In this way the ten blessings also correspond to the Ten Commandments of Moses.

Therefore, the Beatitudes are not only based on the Ten Commandments, they are also the completion of the Ten Commandments. At the same time, they open up a new realm of life according to the Ten Commandments. They show that Jesus had a deep understanding of human nature. It is only through the purification of the soul that a person may fulfill the commandments of God and live a new life in God. Poverty in spirit, which begins the Beatitudes, provides the solution and liberation of the covetousness of the human heart and lays the spiritual foundation of the Ten Commandments.

The Beatitudes are not only a standard for dealing with people, but also encapsulate an ethical attitude to life. It is the attitude with which Jesus lived his own life and the natural expression of Jesus' love and compassion. The Beatitudes start from poverty, symbolizing that the incarnated Son became poor for our sake, and ends with those "who are persecuted for righteousness," symbolizing the persecution of Jesus on the cross at the end of his life. Therefore, the Beatitudes are the eight paths of the Christian life to the Son of God, who lived briefly on earth. If the life of Jesus is said to be a diamond, then the state of life described by the Beatitudes reflects eight aspects of that life; all reflect the face of Jesus. In this Christmas season, we come to meditate on the Beatitudes as if we come to the mirror of Jesus to look at our lives. We stand in front of eight (or ten) portraits of Jesus, so that the new life in us can imitate him and love him.

People who live in this age of clamor will be confused most of the time when reading the Beatitudes. The blessings Jesus pronounced are not what we would expect. We aspire to be arrogant, not meek. We want to be rich, not poor. We want to be euphoric, not to mourn. We want to eat to our heart's contend, not be hungry. We want to succeed, not to be persecuted. But when Jesus began his preaching, he immediately stated the blessings in a clear and unambiguous way. It was to let us meditate on the true meaning of life and the way Christians may achieve blessedness.

The theme of the first blessing is poverty. Matthew differs from Luke in that the former reads "poor in spirit," which is translated in the Chinese Union Version as "the humble," whereas the latter refers to the poor in terms of a person's social position and economic status. The basic meaning of poverty is the lack of essentials to sustain material life: hunger, misfortune, and hardship. The poor are often bullied and insulted and live on the margins of society. In the Old Testament era, the Israelites, for the most part, lived in a weak state and were oppressed by various world empires. The experience of being slaves in Egypt shaped their self-consciousness. But God rescued them from Egypt, and they became a free people. Therefore, a consistent theme in the Old Testament is that Yahweh is the God of the poor. In the Law of Moses, the Israelites were required to observe the Sabbath year because "The Sabbath of the land shall provide food for you, for yourself and for your male and female slaves and for your hired worker and the sojourner who lives with you" (Lev 25:6). The Lord "executes justice for the fatherless and the widow, and loves the sojourner, giving him food and clothing" (Deut 10:18). The entire legal system of the Old Testament, with fairness and justice as the highest principles, was also designed to protect the rights of the poor. In this sense, Luke says, "Blessed are you who are poor, for yours is the kingdom of God" (Luke 6:20). This shows that Jesus brought the kingdom of God to the world in which the poor will be protected.

However, God's salvation is not determined by one's economic and social situation. God looks at the heart. The reason why poor people can receive the blessing of heaven is because they generally are more willing to transform themselves spiritually. They are not so proud to think they determine their own destiny. They are not confident in their own abilities. In the face of the call of the kingdom of God, they respond spiritually. Therefore, "the poor in spirit" refers to those who are modest and humble. In the Jewish culture of that time, the word "poor" was often synonymous with *hasid*, or "the pious." As it says in James 2:5, "Listen, my beloved brothers, has not God chosen those who are poor in the world to be rich in faith and heirs of the kingdom, which he has promised to those who love him?" They are humble in their hearts and they can respond to the grace of God with faith and enter the heavenly love of God. Therefore, the poverty mentioned in the Gospel of Luke and the Gospel of Matthew relate to two different aspects of poverty; they are not contradictory but complement each other.

During his life in the world, Jesus displayed a model of poverty in both aspects. In terms of economic and social status, he was poor. He had no house, no land or vineyards, and often suffered hunger. In Matthew 8:20 Jesus says, "Foxes have holes, and birds of the air have nests, but the Son of Man has nowhere to lay his head." He came to earth; he also had no close relatives or friends. However, the poverty he demonstrated as the supreme paradigm was his humility of spirit. He had the image of God, but he was completely self-effacing, hiding his divinity, and taking the form of a servant. It seemed he had no power, no wisdom, no glory. This was complete poverty. He not only had nothing, but even lost his own life in the end. As Gregory of Nyssa once said, "With respect to the Lord, what greater poverty is there than taking on the form of a servant? With respect to the king of the universe, what is humbler than sharing in our pitiable human nature?"[1] If it was only for the sake of material poverty, Jesus may not have been as severe as the Essenes, who lived in the desert near the Dead Sea, or not as good as John the Baptist, who wore camel's hair as clothing and ate wild honey and locusts. But Jesus' spiritual humility and real poverty in life point to an inner motivation that makes his poverty of supreme importance. In 2 Corinthians 8:9 Paul pointed out the meaning of his poverty: "For you know the grace of our Lord Jesus Christ, that though he was rich, yet for your sake he became poor, so that you by his poverty might become rich." The poverty of Jesus is the expression of his love.

So, today, how do we follow Jesus and how do we imitate his poverty? To imitate Jesus' poverty means to follow Jesus in living a modest life. Jesus used his poverty to show us how to manage the relationship between our hearts and external objects. Those who enter the kingdom of heaven are those who are poor and those whose hearts are not subject to possessions. Those who live in poverty, those who pursue a simple life, know that they are only passing through this world. They understand that everything in the world is a created entity. It cannot be used to fill the human heart and mind, and neither should it become the master of life. Living a simple life exercises the mind not to get attached to material objects. To live a life of voluntary poverty is to make a silent but firm declaration to the world: this world will pass away, and the eternal dwelling of Christians is not in this world. It is the land far away that attracts the pilgrim.

Living a simple life also demonstrates Christian responsibility towards others and nature. In today's world, people have become slaves to a consumer culture. The value of a person seems to lie in how much wealth he or she possesses, or how many items he or she consumes. People have become slaves to commodity fetishism. With his poverty, Jesus reminded us of the value of a prudent and modest life in this frenzy consumer culture. As Saint Francis once said to his followers, "You are to be satisfied with what the

---

1. Gregory of Nyssa, "The Beatitudes," 91.

Lord has given us. If you go beyond necessity, if you go and get it and use it, you are in fact stealing it. You always need to take a little less than what you need, so as not to take that which is your brother's part."[2] In today's deteriorating ecological environment, the excessive gathering of possessions not only reduces other people's property, it is also stealing from the lives of future generations.

If poverty only expresses the relationship between people and things, then it is only a neutral concept. With less material possessions, people can still enjoy happiness. The simple life makes people free. However, in reality poverty is often the result of human sin. People deprive other people of their basic needs because of their greed or exploitation. Furthermore, sinful human beings often defy, insult, and bully the poor through political, legal, and violent means through the inequality of possessions. Against this background, Christians should follow Jesus' poverty by emptying themselves and becoming poor, imitating Jesus, who became poor for us and who carried our diseases. Disciples will use the love of Jesus to identify those in the crowd who are poor, who have been bullied, and who have suffered misfortune, and embrace them in love, because our Lord was once one of these poor people. It does not matter how insignificant our actions appear; we will have a rich treasure in heaven, for they are done for the Lord.

PRAYER

Lord Jesus, you emptied yourself and took the form of a servant to save us. You came into the world in poverty and opened the deepest mysteries of heaven and earth to us. We pray that you come and live in us, that we may live out your life of humility and poverty.

You were born in poverty, but you treated people with gentleness. Make us to be instruments for your use, to comfort those who are poor and humble, and to receive the eternal joy that you promised to humanity.

Lord Jesus, through your coming, you have already injected the power of redemption into the world. We pray that you will continually instill the breath of life into the world of poverty and brokenness as the light of the blind, the power of the weak, and the comfort of the afflicted.

Amen.

---

2. Brother Leo of Assisi, *Mirror of Perfection*, 20.

15

Those Who Mourn

SCRIPTURE

"Blessed are those who mourn, for they shall be comforted" (Matt 5:4)

"Blessed are you who weep now, for you shall laugh . . . Woe to you who laugh now, for you shall mourn and weep." (Luke 6:21, 25)

QUESTIONS

1. What value does mourning have in life? What is the spiritual meaning of sorrow for Christians?
2. How does Jesus' sorrow and joy correspond to the sorrow and joy of our ancestor Adam?
3. How many times did Jesus weep on earth? What does it show on each occasion?
4. Why should Christians mourn? What is the significance for us of Peter's sorrow after the rooster crowed?

MEDITATION

In the first beatitude, Jesus blesses those who are poor; in the second, he blesses those who mourn. The second beatitude refers to one of the most basic human emotional experiences: sorrow and joy. In all the Beatitudes of Jesus there is a tension between the actual and what should be, between the present situation and the future destiny. This tension enables us to reflect on the true meaning of life and to examine our hope for the future. In light of our current life situation, the Beatitudes emphasize the reversal of fortunes.

The Beatitudes refer not only to the life of Jesus, but also to the life of every Christian. As they all refer to Jesus himself, they emphasize the incarnation of Jesus and the transformation of human destiny. In terms of their significance for the lives of every Christian, they mean a complete transformation of life because of the gospel.

Rejoicing or mourning is the direct emotional expression of the human mind as it touches the world. Sorrow and joy reflect the condition of the human heart. Losing or gaining what people treasure translates into sorrow or joy. But sorrow and joy are not separate entities. They are two aspects of the same thing and they represent the yin and yang of the way of life. The Bible tells us that there are two prototypes of sorrow and joy: one is the sorrow and joy of Adam and Eve and the other is the sorrow and joy of Jesus.

God created Adam and Eve according to his "image and likeness" and placed them in the garden of Eden to enjoy the blessedness of fellowship with God. But under the temptation of the devil, Eve "saw that the tree was good for food, and that it was a delight to the eyes, and that the tree was to be desired to make one wise" (Gen 3:6), and then, contrary to God's command, she plucked the fruit and shared it with Adam. The fruit was pleasing to their eyes, good for food, and made them happy, but the enjoyment of eating it was followed by the pain of being expelled from the garden, hard labor, and the battle between the sexes. Adam and Eve used to be a happy couple, but they came to mourn and cry. The pain of death like a descending dark cloud overshadowed their laughter. But then the Word became flesh and Jesus began the work of redemption in the world. He wept over the mortal destiny of man (John 11:35) and cried out in agony on the cross (Mark 15:34). But his great grief brought great joy to humanity. From the great sorrow of Jesus, humanity obtained joy, which is above all spiritual; human beings regained their relationship with God. This joy also includes the love between men and women, friendships, peace, and harmony with nature.

"Blessed are those who mourn, for they shall be comforted" (Matt 5:4). The blessing of Jesus reminds us that mourning and laughing all have their value. Weeping reminds people of the reality of suffering so that people can truly face suffering and its various causes. It makes people mature and strong. Mourning leads people to sympathize with those who suffer. Similarly, Jesus welcomes laughter in life. Joy and celebration appear on every page of the New Testament. The book of Revelation refers to the Lamb's wedding banquet to describe the harmony between God and humanity in Jesus. People celebrate with each other and live in harmony with nature. The laughter condemned by Jesus is selfish and self-centered, a laughter that ridicules others, or a laughter that treats laughter itself as the goal, even at the expense of others' suffering.

Jesus came to the world in the flesh and his humanity was real. He was "a man of sorrows, and acquainted with grief" (Isa 53:3). To understand his beatitude to "those who mourn," one may refer to Jesus himself. His first recorded sorrow was over Jerusalem. According to Luke 19:41 and Matthew 23:37–38, when Jesus came to Jerusalem and saw the city, he mourned for it and said, "O Jerusalem, Jerusalem, the city that kills the prophets and stones those who are sent to it! How often would I have gathered your children together as a hen gathers her brood under her wings, and you were not willing! See, your house is left to you desolate" (Matt 23:37–38). Here Jesus is weeping for the world. Jerusalem symbolized the holiest city and the holiest people in the world. Even so, Jerusalem killed the prophets sent to her, and the "City of Peace" could not obtain peace. Facing a world that was so sinful, blind, and violent, Jesus' mourning expressed his deep love for sinners.

Again, Jesus wept in John 11:33–35: "When Jesus saw her weeping, and the Jews who had come with her also weeping, he was deeply moved in his spirit and greatly troubled. And he said, 'Where have you laid him?' They said to him, 'Lord, come and see.' Jesus wept." In a world where everyone was dying and mourning, Jesus wept like everyone else. The Creator of the universe, in the presence of a man's tomb, did not directly use his power to awaken the dead, but cried like everyone else. What does his mourning mean to us? The mourning of Jesus shows God's love for humanity. In every moment of hardship, Jesus cries with the suffering ones. In the face of sin and death, Jesus did not simply destroy these enemies with his power. Today, difficulties and sorrows are real; Jesus experiences our hardships and sorrows in his true humanity. In his mourning, he invites us to establish a love relationship with him and to walk with him in sorrow. At the same time, he also lets the distressed ones see hope because our affliction is accompanied by his own grief. It convinces people of Jesus' words "Come to me, all who labor and are heavy laden, and I will give you rest" (Matt 11:28). The Lord weeps with us, and so we may be sure, "Blessed are those who mourn, for they shall be comforted." Therefore, the mourning of Jesus in front of Lazarus' tomb also sets a good example for all who wish to become disciples of Jesus. Sorrowing with the needy is the first step in entering the life of others in love.

There is another kind of mourning in the Bible which Jesus did not experience, but it is the mournful cry in the life of every Christian. Jesus took on full humanity, but he did not sin. Therefore, he never had remorse over his own sin. The most classic case of this weeping is Peter:

> Then they seized him and led him away, bringing him into the high priest's house, and Peter was following at a distance. And when they had kindled a fire in the middle of the courtyard and sat down together, Peter sat down among them. Then a servant girl, seeing him as he sat in the light and looking closely at him, said, "This man also was with him." But he denied it, saying, "Woman, I do not know him." And a little later someone else saw him and said, "You also are one of them." But Peter said, "Man, I am not." And after an interval of about an hour still another insisted, saying, "Certainly this man also was with him, for he too is a Galilean." But Peter said, "Man, I do not know what you are talking about." And immediately, while he was still speaking, the rooster crowed. And the Lord turned and looked at Peter. And Peter remembered the saying of the Lord, how he had said to him, "Before the rooster crows today, you will deny me three times." And he went out and wept bitterly. (Luke 22:54–62)

The starting point of repentance is mourning in the heart. There is pain in the heart that shows a heart of iron has been transformed into a heart of flesh and blood. For Christians, the grief of penitence is precisely due to our willingness to participate in Jesus' sorrowful love for sinners. To be precise, the burgeoning consciousness of human sin is not due to the awakening of the heart to the right and wrong of human nature, but is due to the gift of light from the grace of Jesus. It takes the form of enlightenment on the surface, but in essence it is the searching and calling of the Holy Spirit from the top down. Without the grace of the Holy Spirit, without the light revealed by Jesus, how can sinners know that they walk in darkness? Further, after the mourning of repentance, it is only through the guidance and assistance of the Holy Spirit that the Christian can walk in newness of life that is being renewed day by day.

Through the contrition of mourning, we forsake the path of those "who laugh now" that Adam, the ancestor of all ancestors, started, and embark on the path of blessedness of "those who mourn" that began with Jesus. This mourning is a paradox and a mystery. Just when one realizes the darkness of sin, one has already started to walk in the light. When one is mourning for sin, one has begun to receive the grace of Christ and the comfort of the triune God.

PRAYER

Lord Jesus, you are the true light that came into the world to enlighten people. We pray that you would enlighten the people of the world who live in darkness.

We pray for the grace to have a keen heart, to be vigilant against the evil forces of the world, and to cry and walk with those who are harmed by sin.

May you, light of wisdom, shine in us and remind us of the sins we have committed, and may we then mourn. Call on us to enter the kingdom of light and to be courageous to overcome the forces of darkness.

Draw near to us and cleanse us so that we may walk in ever-renewing life through the power of your Spirit. Strengthen our faith in you, revive our hope for salvation, and increase our love for our neighbors.

Amen.

16

The Meek

SCRIPTURE

"Blessed are the meek, for they shall inherit the earth." (Matt 5:5)

"... but in your hearts honor Christ the Lord as holy, always being prepared to make a defense to anyone who asks you for a reason for the hope that is in you; yet do it with gentleness and respect ..." (1 Pet 3:15)

QUESTIONS

1. What does it mean to be "meek"?
2. How did Jesus express meekness during his life?
3. How is the Christian's meekness rooted in the three qualities of the Holy Spirit that come from faith and love? How does one practice meekness in daily life?

MEDITATION

What is meekness? Meekness refers to a person's character, and it is a way of treating others. It refers to a person's inner modesty, which is not self-centered and not lofty. It is the quality that enables us to see other people's

The Meek

strengths, to respect others, and to treat people with courtesy. Therefore, the Old Testament also has a very high appraisal of meekness. Proverbs 15:4 says, "A gentle tongue is a tree of life." Ecclesiasticus 6:5 also reads, "Pleasant words win many friends, and an affable manner makes acquaintance easy." In the evaluation of Moses' life, we note the following statement in Numbers 12:3: "Now the man Moses was very meek, more than all people who were on the face of the earth."

However, the beatitude here does not refer to a gentle character in the general sense. It is Christ-centered. It refers to us as followers of Jesus because Jesus is a model of meekness. It also refers to the meekness of our spiritual interactions with Christ. It is a state of life manifested by Christ living in us.

Jesus used the word "gentle" to describe himself: "Take my yoke upon you, and learn from me, for I am gentle and lowly in heart, and you will find rest for your souls" (Matt 11:29). In his Sermon on the Mount, Jesus always quoted the Mosaic law from the Old Testament because it expresses the principles of fairness and justice, which are foundational for the operation of society. But after citing the Old Testament, Jesus would always say, "But I tell you," challenging Christians to raise their ethical standards to a higher level; for example: "Love your enemies and pray for those who persecute you" (Matt 5:44), and "if anyone would sue you and take your tunic, let him have your cloak as well" (Matt 5:40).

Jesus became flesh and died as an atonement for the sin of all people. His whole life was one of gentleness and meekness. The Servant Songs in Isaiah are a profound depiction of the nature of a life in which he was gentle to the point of dying: "He was oppressed, and he was afflicted, yet he opened not his mouth; like a lamb that is led to the slaughter, and like a sheep" (Isa 53:7). When he died without sin on the cross, he prayed, "Forgive them, for they do not know what they are doing" (Luke 23:34), which was an extreme expression of tenderness to the sinner.

The gentle death of Jesus on the cross reveals to us the other side of the divinity hidden in mystery: tenderness, forgiveness, and non-resistance are signs of God's power. Real power is not to exalt oneself, to surpass others, but to humble oneself, to serve others, and to exalt others. Here, Jesus' tribute to gentleness subverts people's mundane imaginations of victory, power, and glory. In the world a general achieves success on the dry bones of thousands, and secular history celebrates the glory of heroes but forgets the sacrifice of others. Jesus on the cross understood that to be the real victor one had to become the victim.

The meek "will inherit the earth" because they are not following the logic of the strong man in this world, but they use heaven's law as a rule of life. They will join Jesus in the promised land of eternal life; the meek will win the hearts of people through their words and deeds. The hearts of others is the "earth" won by the meek. The meek stand by themselves and with those who are being exploited, who have no voice and who are disrespected. The meek see Jesus in the face of the poor. They are gathering together from the four corners of the world; "those who wait on the Lord will inherit the earth" (Ps 37:9).

For Christians, meekness is not the virtue of our own power, but comes from the gift that the triune God has given us. It is one of the "fruits of the Spirit" (Gal 5:22). It is a reward that Christ has earned for us, as stated in Colossians 3:12: "Put on then, as God's chosen ones, holy and beloved, compassionate hearts, kindness, humility, meekness, and patience."

Meekness stems from the three virtues of the Christian life: faith, hope, and love. First of all, it comes directly from our deep faith in Christ. Confidence allows us to "consecrate Christ" in our hearts." In biblical tradition, "consecration" means that the object of reverence or holiness is completely separated from the world. To consecrate Christ or to honor Christ as holy is to thoroughly differentiate between Christ's ways and worldliness in faith. It is to follow the lifestyle of Jesus and to imitate his meekness to the exclusion of any secular factors and considerations. Secondly, meekness also stems from the hope that is in the Christian's heart. The heart is filled with the hope of eternal life and the kingdom of God. With this hope, we can forget those things that are behind and reach forth unto those things that are ahead (Phil 3:13). In a world full of violence and hatred, Christians may answer everyone with a gentle heart. In the end, meekness is a manifestation of divine love and righteousness. Meek people are not hypocrites and they do not discard righteous anger. When Jesus was slapped in the face when cross-examined by the high priest, he did not turn his left cheek to be slapped as well. Instead, he rightly denounced him: "When he had said these things, one of the officers standing by struck Jesus with his hand, saying, 'If what I said is wrong, bear witness about the wrong; but if what I said is right, why do you strike me?'" (John 18:23). But meekness can control anger and enable believers to face sinners in peace and righteousness.

It enables people to hate sin but to love the sinner, to treat sinners as equals, and to respect the dignity and personality of those who make mistakes.

Like other character traits, meekness is one of the results of the Christian spiritual life. It is a union of human nature with divinity, which enables the inner self to remain in the Word. It is not confined to a few clergy but should be practiced by every disciple of Jesus; it is not limited to certain specific occasions or moments, but should naturally be revealed in the details of everyday life. Both the Western Christian tradition and China's indigenous culture have provided us with rich insights and practical resources on meekness.

Living in seventeenth-century France, Lawrence (1614–1691) was an ordinary handyman in a monastery. He was a coachman, a kitchen hand, and later a shoemaker. After his death, his letters and conversations were compiled into a small book, *The Practice of the Presence of God*. In his opinion, God is at our side always and everywhere. Therefore, whether collecting wood or water, one should always pray. He wrote, "In the noise of the kitchen, when many people wanted me to do different things at the same time, I had God on my side. I calmly prayed to him as if I were in front of him in the holiest communion."[1] Prayer does not require a quiet place, nor much preparation. There is no more important thing than prayer, and there is no easier thing than prayer. By simply raising your heart, a little bit of concentration, and a bit of immersion in the love of God, you can talk to God. For Christians, prayer is to talk softly with Jesus in the heart. A meek person before God can create an inner world that is totally unrelated to and independent of the external environment.

The practice of meekness before God is from moment to moment, in every little thing, and in every activity of the day. God is found in everything. Be accustomed to being with God and getting joy from it. Always, in every moment of life, speak to Jesus humbly. To talk with him affectionately, there is no need to follow any rules or procedures. This is true when we are tempted, when we are suffering, when we are tired and bored, and even when our confidence is shaken, and our hearts are weak. To practice meekness is also to develop a kind of life that follows the course of nature, to accept everything God has arranged for our lives. Lawrence thus said, "As long as God is willing, we are willing to suffer. The one who suffers with God is happy. To be accustomed to suffering, just pray to God for the power to endure suffering. Accept illness and disease and regard it as grace

---

1. Brother Lawrence, *Practice of the Presence of God*, 14.

coming from God. Bitterness comes from God's hands and is God's way to save us."[2]

To practice meekness before God is to take a different path from the world. It is a way that goes against the traffic, and it is the "Little Way." Saint Therese of Lisieux reminded people to say, "I don't want to climb a spiritual ladder. I just want to find a straight ladder that can take me up. I'm too weak to climb a winding sacred ladder. I don't want to be someone big. I only want Jesus' hand to lift me to heaven." She also said, "You want to climb a high mountain, but God just wants you to go down. He is waiting for you in the humble valley!"[3]

Interestingly, the Chinese Union Version chose the two characters *wen* (温) and *rou* (柔) for the translation of the Greek word πραΰς (*praus*, the meek). We may use the characters *wen*, meaning "warm," and *rou*, meaning "soft," to meditate on their association with the teachings of Jesus. The character 温 (*wen*) is based on the character for water, and water is the perfect interpretation of Jesus' character. Laozi once said, "The highest excellence is like (that of) water. The excellence of water appears in its benefiting all things, and in its occupying, without striving (to the contrary), the low place which all men dislike. Hence (its way) is near to (that of) the Dao."[4] The general idea is that the greatest good is like water. Water can be beneficial to all things, but it does not compete. It is willing to do what no one wants to do and resembles the Way. Lao Tzu also used the image of water to remind us of the position of the rivers and ocean in the natural world. He said: "Why is the sea king of a hundred streams? Because it lies below them. Therefore, it is the king of a hundred streams."[5] Jesus was the ruler of all things, but he humbled himself in order to save humanity and came into the world veiling his power. Like water, he walked down, took the form of a servant, and was despised and crucified. He also encouraged his disciples to be like him, like water flowing down the river, to serve and not to be served.

Confucius also liked to observe water and deduced eleven virtues from the water. They can also be used as a description of Jesus. He said:

> When water spreads all over the world, gives all things, and is not selfish, it is like a gentleman's morality. Wherever it goes,

---

2. Brother Lawrence, *Practice of the Presence of God*, 21.
3. Feduccia, ed., "Selections from *The Story of a Soul*," 153.
4. Lao-Tzu, *Tao Teh King*, ch. 8.
5. Lao-Tzu, *Tao Teh King*, ch. 66.

The Meek

everything grows, like a gentleman's kindness. Water naturally flows down and is shaped by its environment, like a gentleman's impartiality. It flows in the shallows and also fills the depths, like a gentleman's wisdom. It rushes into a gorge without hesitation, like a gentleman's decisiveness and courage. It seeps into the smallest fissures and reaches everywhere, like a gentleman's comprehensive understanding. Even when criticized, water remains silent, like the gentleman's inclusiveness. When it mixes with mud and sand, in the end, it is still clear water, like a gentleman is goodness at transforming things. After filling a measuring device it remains a level, like a gentleman's uprightness. When it is full, it is not greedy for more, like a gentleman who pays attention to his sense of proportion. No matter what kind of obstacle it faces, it continues to flow east into the sea, like a gentleman's unwavering faith and will.[6]

We may observe the following points: (1) Only when there is water can there be life; water nourishes everything, treats everything unselfishly, just as Jesus loves everyone. (2) All things that come into contact with water can grow and survive, just as with Jesus' benevolent heart. (3) Water flows downwards and is in accordance with the principles of all things encountered, just like Jesus' impartiality. (4) Water flows in shallow places, but in the depths it is like a deep gorge beyond measure, like the wisdom of Jesus. (5) Even if we rush into the gorge, the water will not waver, just as Jesus' determination. 6) Water infiltrates into every small fissure, just as Jesus' insight into human nature. (7) Water doesn't object to getting dirty, just as Jesus associated with sinners. (8) Water can engulf unclean things, but the it cleanses them, just as Jesus was good at influencing and healing sinners. (9) After water fills a container, it remains level, just like the integrity of Jesus. (10) When water has filled a container, it is not greedy for more things, just like the contentment of Jesus. (11) No matter what kind of twists or hardships, water flows eastwards, just like Jesus' determination to accomplish God's plan of redemption.

The character 柔 (*rou*), meaning "soft," also has a profound meaning in Chinese cultural traditions. Laozi treats softness as the basic characteristic of water, but the strongest thing in the world cannot overcome the softness of water. He said: "There is nothing in the world softer and weaker than water, and yet for attacking things that are firm and strong there is nothing that can take precedence of it; for there is nothing (so effectual) for which it can be changed. Everyone in the world knows that the soft

---

6. Liu Xiang, "Conversation between Confucius and Zi Gong," 434–35.

overcomes the hard, and the weak the strong, but no one is able of carrying it out in practice."[7] The weak is strong; that is indeed the faith shown by Jesus on the cross. He also said: "The softest thing in the world dashes against and overcomes the hardest."[8] This is also derived from the meditation on water. Water is the most delicate thing, but it can rush out of the earth and form rivers, and perpetual drops of water can penetrate hard rocks, just as the gospel of Jesus can occupy the hearts of people because of its softness, leading to the establishment of strong and lasting churches to transform this dark world. The wisdom of the weak overcoming the strong realized by Lao Tzu is echoed in the apostle Paul's interpretation of Jesus' identity: "the weakness of God is stronger than men" (1 Cor 1:25). Lao Tzu also said: "Man at his birth is supple and weak; at his death, firm and strong."[9] Softness is a feature of life and rigidity is a feature of death. The gentleness of Jesus is the sign that God's life is operating on the earth.

PRAYER

Lord Jesus, you humbly came to earth; meekly you accepted the divine plan to save us and to sanctify us.

You are the righteousness Father God has placed upon us. May the seeds of righteousness, love. and meekness sprout in our lives.

You came to heal broken hearts. Use your meekness to heal the wounds of our hearts. Let us treat each other with your meekness.

We pray that you help us be meek toward everything around us, believe that everything comes out of your will, and find your will in all the things.

Amen.

---

7. Lao-Tzu, *Tao Teh King*, ch. 78.
8. Lao-Tzu, *Tao Teh King*, ch. 43.
9. Lao-Tzu, *Tao Teh King*, ch. 76.

17

Those Who Thirst for Righteousness

SCRIPTURE

"Blessed are those who hunger and thirst for righteousness, for they shall be satisfied." (Matt 5:6)

"Jesus said to her, 'Everyone who drinks of this water will be thirsty again, but whoever drinks of the water that I will give him will never be thirsty again. The water that I will give him will become in him a spring of water welling up to eternal life.'" (John 4:13–14)

QUESTIONS

1. How can we pray for God's righteousness with hunger and thirst? Before we long for God's righteousness, what does God desire from us?

2. What do we mean by "God's righteousness"? How does God's righteousness manifest in our relationship with God, in our relationships with others, and in our relationship with the environment?

3. In the last day, at our wedding with the Lamb, our hunger and thirst will be fully satisfied. But in order to drink with Christ, how should we treat the hungry people around us in this world?

MEDITATION

Everyone experiences hunger and thirst in life. The hungry seek food and the thirsty seek water. This is natural for humans. In the fourth beatitude, Jesus blesses those who hunger and thirst for righteousness. In meditating on this text, we need to ask ourselves, how do we pray for God's righteousness with a hungry and thirsty heart? What is righteousness? Who are the hungry around us? How should we treat them?

Confucius once exclaimed, "I have not seen one who loves virtue as he loves beauty."[1] Morality and justice are spiritual pursuits, whereas sex, food, and drink are basic needs for survival. As far as the goal of human spiritual civilization is concerned, the pursuit of righteousness is endless; it is long and continuous. But in terms of survival, the pursuit of food and water is most primitive, passionate, and strong. The hungry and thirsty ones are those who consider the spiritual pursuit as the most basic need of life; they are those eager to see the face of God in a primitive and direct way.

In the fourth chapter of the Gospel of John, the encounter between Jesus and the Samaritan woman reveals the mystery of how "those who hunger and thirst for righteousness" will be satisfied. The longing for God in each of us is the longing that God placed in our hearts when he created us. Every thirsty person, as the Samaritan women who went to fetch water, must come to the well and meet with Christ. In fact, when we ask Jesus for water, he also begins to ask us for water to drink. It was he who first said, "Please give me water to drink" (John 4:7). This shows that when we were looking for him, Christ had already come to seek us. His search for us comes from the depths of God's heart: God longing for us. Therefore, the essence of our faith lies in our thirst for God: our longing for God and God's longing for us meet together. In other words, in our longing for God, God's desire for us is implied. God longs for us to long for him. Therefore, Jesus said, "Ask, and it will be given to you; seek, and you will find; knock, and it will be opened to you. For everyone who asks receives, and the one who seeks finds, and to the one who knocks it will be opened" (Matt 7:7–8). The supplication implies that the opening is implicit in the knocking, and fullness is hidden in hunger and thirst.

Those who hunger and thirst for righteousness will connect directly with Christ as the source of righteousness. At the same time, they will also be satisfied in the reconciliation of God and humanity brought about by

---

1. *Analects, Zi Han*, in Legge, trans., *Chinese Classics*, 222.

Christ. The "righteousness" Jesus referred to in the fourth beatitude refers to what he himself said. In this sense, his words that those who hunger and thirst for righteousness will be satisfied are both a current blessing to the disciples as well as a promise of their future salvation. Jesus is our righteousness and the basis of our justification before God. The incarnation of Jesus fulfilled the great exchange project of God. He delivered himself over and died on the cross. He paid the ransom for our sins. At the same time, he gave us divine life so that we could share in the divine nature and enjoy communion with God in eternal life. The night before his death, Jesus also instituted the communion meal, using wine and bread to represent his blood and flesh, which satisfy the hunger and thirst of those on the way heaven.

It is necessary that a person who hungers and thirsts for righteousness remembers the advice Jesus had given: "You shall love the Lord your God with all your heart and with all your soul and with all your mind. This is the great and first commandment. And a second is like it: You shall love your neighbor as yourself. On these two commandments depend all the Law and the Prophets" (Matt 22:37–40). The first is the vertical dimension of righteousness and the second is the horizontal dimension of righteousness. The command to "love your neighbor as yourself" requires that "those who hunger and thirst for righteousness" care for those who physically hunger and thirst.

Jesus became a human being and died on the cross. The righteousness of Christ not only straightened out our vertical relationship with God and corrected our horizontal relationship with our neighbors, it also has an ecological significance by reminding us how to deal rightly with nature. The significance of Christ's coming, suffering, and salvation incorporates all of creation. As Romans 8:22 says, because of humanity's sin and rebellion, "we know that the whole creation has been groaning together in the pains of childbirth until now." The apostle Paul realized nearly two thousand years ago that the earth, the sky, and all living things have been contaminated by human sin and are in distress. Two thousand years later, especially in modern times, "the whole creation" has sunk deeper into sighs and hardships. As human science and technology continue to advance, the ability to change and control nature has greatly increased, but human spirituality has not been improved. Through the advancement of power, evils such as greed and oppression are amplified, and the harmful impact of humans upon nature is also increasing. Under the stimulation of a consumer culture, nature has become riddled with pollution. Waste and pollution have brought substantial and persistent damage to the earth, atmosphere, and water. Clean drinking water resources continue to disappear. There is also a constant decline in biodiversity. Every year, thousands of species disappear, both flora and fauna. Global warming is causing extreme weather conditions.

People once thought that our negative impact upon nature would be alleviated through technological progress. People did not realize that every human intervention in nature involves sinful human genes. Sophisticated technology often brings greater and newer toxicity. Moreover, institutions are driven by commercial interests and consumerism. Without the change of the inner soul, every wave of scientific and technological progress only makes our nature less rich, less beautiful, paler, and weaker.

Romans 8:19–26 enables us to understand the ecological significance of the righteousness of Christ. Its themes include solidarity between humanity and nature in sighs and labors and hope through the Spirit in Christ. The disobedience of Adam corrupted everything that was originally considered by God to be "very good" (Gen 1:31). The rebellion of Adam subjected all creation, which God regarded as good, to corruption. We who are covered by the righteousness of Christ, that is, the "firstfruits of the Spirit" (Rom 8:23), cannot place ourselves outside the natural world, but should regard ourselves as members of nature and as repairers and caretakers (Gen 2:15) who sigh and groan with all things in nature. Since we are involved in the groans of all things, we may also bring hope to all things. "Likewise the Spirit helps us in our weakness. For we do not know what to pray for as we ought, but the Spirit himself intercedes for us with groanings too deep for words" (Rom 8:26). The Holy Spirit participates in the sighs of humanity and creation. He also brings the hope in Christ into the natural world. Christ, who entered this world, also carried the burden of the living things of nature and his resurrection also brought healing and salvation to nature.

Maintaining an attitude of oneness for all things in nature is an intrinsic part of what it means to hunger and thirst for righteousness. Care for nature is an intrinsic part of our communion with Christ and is a means of witnessing to Christ's righteousness in the world. It means that we love the universe with Christ and suffer with Christ in all things. The suffering, unity, and action that are united with all things in Christ are part of the Holy Spirit's work of sanctification in us. In this way, we also show the world the power of Christ and demonstrate to people the hope of renewing everything in Christ.

The righteousness of Christ is not only for us; it is also for our neighbors and for the chaotic world around us. It requires us not simply to say "amen" to Jesus' blessings, but also to expand our realm of life. This is also why we want to be benevolent people who integrate heaven and earth with everything as in the Chinese cultural tradition. The Ming Confucian scholar Wang Yangming (1472–1529) once said that the real gentleman ("Great Man," *Da Ren*) is a person who has become one with all things in the world. He regards the world as a family and treats the entire human race as one. Those who separate you and me from other things are actually villains ("Little man," *Xiao Ren*). This type of benevolent person who embraces all things does not consciously go out to do something good, but his or her actions are a natural expression of the inner heart. This kind of person, on the spiritual level, is in touch with the spirit of heaven and earth. On the social level, when seeing people suffer, they will display much compassion since they are at one with the weak and the poor. On the ecological level, when seeing the mourning of animals and the destruction of vegetation, they will not be indifferent but will express concern since they are at one with the birds, animals, and vegetation. On the natural level, even when seeing the destruction of the stone, they will feel pity, since they are even at one with the stone. According to *Inquiry into the Great Learning* by Wang Yangming, this kind of feeling or compassion towards all things in heaven and earth is the sigh that the Holy Spirit affects in the hearts of those who hunger and thirst for righteousness.[2]

The disciples of Christ are hungry because they have been pursuing the feast of drinking with Christ. Today, we are grateful for the food that God has given to everyone. In the future, we will enjoy the wedding with Christ in the New Jerusalem. The feast of the last day is for us, but we must go through the middle of a field where we need to share all we have and provide for the hungry people in the world, to feed the hungry, to give drink to the thirsty, to clothe the naked, to host travelers, to take care of the sick, to visit prisoners, to bury the dead (Matt 25:35–40), until they become one with all things that are hungry.

---

2. Wang Yangming, *Inquiry into the Great Learning*, 967.

PRAYER

Oh Lord Jesus, you are the source of the joy, bread, and wine of life, and we now cry to you. Lord come, satisfy the hunger and thirst of our lives.

The world was your vineyard but became a desert because of sin. We pray that you will pour out your Spirit to water the lifeless world.

You want all people to be gathered into the kingdom of God. May they feel the thirst for your word and be satisfied with your bread of life.

You are the deep. We call on you from our depths; we pray that you move us to thirst for you and satisfy our thirst for you through our prayer.

Amen.

18

The Merciful

SCRIPTURE

"Blessed are the merciful, for they shall receive mercy." (Matt 5:7)

"And he cried out, 'Jesus, Son of David, have mercy on me!'" (Luke 18:38; cf. Matt 20:30–31)

QUESTIONS

1. What is the relationship between the poverty of the first beatitude and the mercy of the fifth beatitude?
2. Why is mercy related to God's name? Why does Jesus' death on the cross reveal God's mercy?
3. How is mercy the source of human empathy, shame, respect, and discernment?

MEDITATION

The Beatitudes can be divided into two sections. The first four blessings describe how Jesus takes care of those in need and the last four blessings describe how the faithful walk with Jesus. But they are all centered on Jesus;

that is to say, it is Jesus' character and actions that give these eight blessings their meaning and value. It is also only through Jesus that these eight blessings can transform our lives.

The Greek term for "merciful" in the fifth beatitude may also be translated as "compassionate." as translated in the Chinese Union Version of the Bible. In the famous Jesus Prayer in Matthew 20:30–31, the verb "have mercy" is used. The term is used widely in the Bible and has been rendered into different Chinese words, and each of them has a profound meaning in Chinese cultural history. If the first four blessings begin with poverty, then the last four blessings begin with mercy. These are exactly the two opposite ends of the gospel of Christ: our poverty calls for God's infinite mercy. Only in poverty can we truly honor God, pray for his mercy, receive his mercy, and celebrate his mercy.

Mercy is the name of God, reflecting his gracious nature (Exod 34:6). The main emphasis of the Bible, whether in the Old Testament or the New Testament, is on God's love. When the Israelite poet explains the origin of the world and recalls everything the Israelites experienced, he simply repeats the refrain "for his mercy endures forever" (Ps 136). God responds to Israel and to the poverty, the suffering, and the need of all creation by his loving-kindness. In loving-kindness, God also experiences joy (Mic 7:18). In other words, loving-kindness brings divine joy.

In his sermon, Jesus pointed out that kindness is an attribute of the Father: "Be merciful, even as your Father is merciful" (Luke 6:36). When Jesus completed his mission in the world, the disciples around him became more fully aware that in the person of Jesus God's heart was opened up. His mercy was clearly revealed to the world. Jesus was born as a human being and brought God's mercy to the suffering world. Jesus is the embodiment of compassion. He walked with the blind, the lame, and the lepers, and with his power he led them into a new kind of life. He created new possibilities where there were none and opened up paths where there were none. Finally, after being judged, he was crucified. Jesus on the cross is the greatest demonstration of God's compassion for the world. Because Jesus compassionately bore all the sin of people in his wounds, they may now also be partakers of his resurrection and receive eternal life.

The church made up of Christians does not have any reason to boast of itself. The splendor on the face of the church reflects the glory of the love of Christ in heaven. The gospel preached by the church merely announces God's mercy to humanity; the sacraments the church performs, whether

The Merciful

baptism or Holy Communion, disseminate the power of the love of the Holy Spirit.

"Blessed are the merciful, for they shall receive mercy" (Matt 5:7) has the same meaning as the Lord's Prayer, which we recite every day: "forgive us our debts, as we also have forgiven our debtors" (Matt 6:12). Just as Jesus said, "if you do not forgive others their trespasses, neither will your Father forgive your trespasses" (Matt 6:15). It is in God's nature to show compassion. When a person has compassion for others, he or she is imitating Christ. The merciful is the one who has "put on" Christ (Gal 3:27), revealing his or her identity as a child of God. Those who are merciful "shall receive mercy." Being able to show mercy to others means recognizing that the person has already received mercy from God. Of course, the showing of mercy must not be regarded as the condition for receiving mercy from God. Grace always takes the first step and our extension of mercy to others is nothing more than a response to God's mercy. If we cannot treat people with compassion, it means that God's mercy has not been effective in us; as shown in Matthew 6:15, God may even withdraw his compassion from us.

The English term "mercy" comes from the Latin *misericordia* ("mercy" is from old French *merci*, which in turn stems from the Latin *merces*); *miseri* means "unfortunate" or "misery," and *cordia* is the human heart, so the original meaning of mercy and compassion is that the heart is stirred by the misfortune of others. One has compassion when one's heart is moved by the plight of another. The showing of compassion is the beginning of the breaking down of human isolation and the closure of the mutual breach between people. A compassionate heart enables us to see the face of God in the face of others, instead of viewing others as a means or a tool to achieve our goals. Compassion breaks the boundaries between us and others, it opens our heart, and it enables us joyfully to let another person enter our world and life. Through compassion we no longer see another person as an instrumental "it" but as a human being in equal relationship with us. Without compassion, mercy, and forgiveness, it will be impossible to build a harmonious society. Society will only be trapped in a vicious cycle of aggression, violence, and mutual harm.

Those who treat others with compassion will receive mercy from God. This is not to say that we can use our compassion as a good work to earn God's compassion, but it allows us to understand that love is indivisible. If we do not love the brothers and sisters who are around us, how can we love the Father, who is far away in heaven? How can you love an invisible God if you cannot love someone whom you can see? Compassion is the agitation of our hearts. Fundamentally speaking, our compassion is not our own, but it comes from the stimulation of the Holy Spirit from the depths of our lives, who transforms the heart by Christ's compassion for all beings. Therefore, this beatitude is a universal blessing for all creatures. Through compassion, humanity with God and people among themselves can be unified, as stated in Ephesians 4:32: "Be kind to one another, tender-hearted, forgiving one another, as God in Christ forgave you."

Compassion is a unity. It includes both God's compassion for people and people's compassion for others. Compassion is the result of our having the mind of Christ (see Phil 2:5). It is the source for all the immanent human virtues. To use Confucian terminology, just as a person as a whole has four limbs, the inner mercy of the human heart appears in four forms: empathy, shame, respectfulness, and discernment. Mencius referred to these as "the four moral instincts,"[1] but they are in fact the manifestations of Christian compassion in different living situations.

The so-called *empathetic heart* refers to the sympathy that we express when we see others in trouble, which translates into actions that care for others. Mencius once gave the following example: when you see that a child is about to fall into a well, you would just instinctively rush to grab him. The action comes directly from the heart, not from any external honor or utilitarian considerations. The virtue of benevolence stems from here.

The so-called *shameful heart*, which is produced by the nourishment of the Holy Spirit, is the sense of shame that Christians develop. Pope Francis I once talked about shame; he said, "We must ask God for the grace of shame, because it is a great grace to be ashamed of our sins and thus receive forgiveness and the generosity to give it to others."[2] Shame is generated in the human heart under the illumination of the Holy Spirit, and it is the action of personal cleansing. Shame brings about the turning of the soul, which in practice manifests itself as repentance and walking in the path of righteousness.

Those with a *respectful heart* are able to see the image of God in the face of each individual. People are located in specific social structures. They have different roles with respect to other people: some are in high positions; some are in low positions; some are rich and some are poor. Jesus did not abolish these social differences, but he demanded that we observe equal

---

1. "Chapter of Gongsunchou I," in Yang Bojun, ed., *Mencius*, 83.
2. Pope Francis, "Grace of Shame."

respect for these social roles while respecting each person's individuality equally. Those in high positions must respect those in low positions; you are to be respected; your deeds must be respected. In a complex society, everyone is sometimes in a high position and sometimes in a low position. However, if everyone treats each other with respect, everyone will feel the warmth of decency even though they live in a society with different classes.

The so-called *discerning heart* can be said to be a synthesis of the previous three. It is a joy to do what is right and a shame to do what is wrong. When God created humanity, he placed the ability to discern right and wrong in the human heart. But sin corrupted this ability. The salvation brought by Christ has both redeemed humans from sin and also lifted the veil on right and wrong. Right and wrong, that is, human conscience, is revealed through the Holy Spirit. Under the illumination of the Holy Spirit, the discerning heart can reflect on how God's law works in all of creation. The discerning heart then gives birth to wisdom. Under the scrutiny of all things, the discerning heart is able to separate right from wrong, which is to live according to wisdom, which makes one more sensitive to the qualities expressed by the empathetic heart, the shameful heart, and the respectful heart.

In this way, with Christ's compassion as the foundation and the extension in the world of life, the Christian sage will live out the virtues of benevolence, righteousness, decency, and wisdom.

PRAYER

Lord Jesus, you are the Son of God. You were at the beginning with God, and you became a man because of God's mercy. May we always be merciful to others.

You became poor so that in our poverty we may become rich in you. You emptied yourself so that our emptiness may be turned into abundance.

You are the light that rises in the morning. Under the light of your truth, may we live a benevolent, righteous, decent, and wise life.

Continue to fill us with your Holy Spirit and let us bear the fruit of good deeds in your mercy.

Amen.

19

The Pure in Heart

SCRIPTURE

"Blessed are the pure in heart, for they shall see God." (Matt 5:8)

"The aim of our charge is love that issues from a pure heart and a good conscience and a sincere faith." (1 Tim 1:5)

QUESTIONS

1. What is a pure heart? How did Jesus demonstrate the power of purity when he faced the three temptations of the devil in the wilderness?
2. Why is the pure heart a gift, a promise, and a mission for us?
3. Why is the pure person able to see the face of God? Where can the pure see God's face?

MEDITATION

In the same way, centering around Jesus, the sixth beatitude brings together two important aspects of the Christian life: having a pure heart and seeing God. Only the pure in heart may see God and seeing God will continually purify a person. This beatitude is related to the two most important rites of the Christian faith: baptism and Communion. Through baptism the Holy Spirit cleanses the heart, and through Communion people come to see the face of Christ and meet with God. The sacraments use common visible things—water and bread—to express the deep and close connection between people and God. Is it not through water and bread that our lives connect with God?

The words in this blessing refer to Jesus: only Jesus is completely pure and only Jesus is the face of God. "No one has ever seen God; the only God, who is at the Father's side, he has made him known" (John 1:18).

What do we mean that Jesus had a pure heart? He dedicated his heart, soul, mind, and strength to his faith in the heavenly Father and strengthened his understanding of his mission through prayer. He expressed the silent power of the kingdom not through an outward display of strength, but through the death of "emptying himself" (Phil 2:7) on the cross. Through this display of power, love prompted the centurion to exclaim, "Truly this was the Son of God!" (Matt 27:54). Jesus showed God's omnipotence to the poor and announced hope to humanity. He loved God with all his heart and used the same heart to love others. He did not repay evil for evil but overcame evil with good. He truly treated people as a purpose, not as a means.

Jesus' purity of mind was not achieved by being removed from temptation, but like ordinary people he experienced temptation. "For we do not have a high priest who is unable to sympathize with our weaknesses, but one who in every respect has been tempted as we are, yet without sin" (Heb 4:15). In his response to Satan's three temptations, he showed us the meaning of having a pure heart. The theme that runs through all of Satan's temptations is the enticement to put the invisible God aside and to trust in what is visible and powerful. In the first temptation, Satan challenged Jesus to turn stones into bread. Food is the most basic need for human survival. Jesus did not deny this. In the miracle of the multiplication of the loaves and fish, he responded to the material needs of thousands of people who followed him into the wilderness. Finally, his death on the cross made him the seed that fell on the ground and die to produce many seeds. Therefore, in his response to Satan, Jesus said, "Man shall not live by bread alone, but by every word that comes from the mouth of God" (Matt 4:4). It means that when we face the temptation of materialism, the priorities of life are crucial. Our highest priority should be to seek God, to listen to his Word, and then to work diligently to share with others. In the face of hunger, Jesus demonstrated his purity. Food is important, but freedom is more valuable; but most important is to be unfailingly loyal to God and to worship him without duplicity.

The ancient Hebrew tradition had a literary habit of inserting a more general paragraph in the middle of two paragraphs with similar meaning. The same is true of the three temptations of Jesus. The temptation that corresponds to the first temptation about food is the third temptation about power. In essence, the third is like the first temptation. The enticement of the temptations is to establish a kingdom that is well developed and abundant in material goods. But Jesus' mission was to be a Suffering Servant, a Messiah who would experience rejection, whipping, and even death. The purpose of Jesus' coming was not to come to realize a specific political system, but instead, through his sufferings and hardships, to enable people to come to see the cruelty of sin and the love of God, and thus to come closer to the true Word, and to establish a quiet, gentle, yet eternal kingdom in the human heart. So, Jesus' third reply was, "Be gone, Satan! For it is written, 'You shall worship the Lord your God and him only shall you serve'" (Matt 4:10). This is a purity shown by Jesus: if people cannot repent by humbling themselves before the Almighty, then any political promise of glory, progress, and prosperity will become the devil's shackle upon humanity.

The second temptation in the middle is more abstract and more general. It sums up the three temptations. Satan tempted Jesus to jump from the top of the temple as the Israelites who had been in the wilderness tested the Lord, "Is the Lord among us or not?" (Exod 17:7). Jesus' answer to Satan points directly to one core issue: "You shall not put the Lord your God to the test" (Matt 4:7). Behind this questioning of God, there is a fundamental assumption that God is an experimental subject. He needs to pass through human tests, like bread and power, in order to be accepted. This is to regard God as part of the created world. People such as the Israelites claim to be higher than God or consider themselves to be God. The rejection of Satan's temptation by Jesus reveals his pure and exclusive dedication to God, which is simply believing, loving, and listening to God.

Jesus' purity of mind was revealed to us more thoroughly during his death on the cross. On the night before his arrest, in his prayer to God in the garden of Gethsemane, even though his human nature was overwhelmed with pain and sorrow, he still prayed to the Father, "Abba, Father, all things are possible for you. Remove this cup from me. Yet not what I will, but what you will" (Mark 14:36). The prayer shows that Jesus is selfless and that he is obedient to the Father's will in everything. When he was crucified, he asked that God forgive those who had crucified him: "Father, forgive them, for they know not what they do" (Luke 23:34). The prayer shows that his heart is selfless and filled with love for the world. His last words on the cross did not contain the slightest grievance or grudge; he simply said "It is finished" in plain and joyful love (John 19:30), showing that his pure heart was completely oblivious of self and was fully occupied with the great mission of worshiping the Father and redeeming the world.

It is because of Jesus' obedience to the heavenly Father's plan of salvation in his pure heart that we sinners can obtain the purity of heaven. For us, a pure heart is a gift, a promise, and a mission. It entails three aspects: it is a gift we receive from God, it is a promise we can finally achieve in the future, and it is also part of our mission in this world.

Our heart becomes clean not through our own efforts, but through the ransom Jesus paid for us on the cross. Purity of heart becomes possible for us through the sacrament of baptism. Baptism symbolizes the forgiveness of sins, it washes away impurity, and it means to be united with the death and resurrection of Christ. Through our faith in Christ, the Holy Spirit created a clean heart in us through baptism. For us, a pure heart is a gift.

Although we have had the soul cleansed before God and sin no longer has power over us, we are still on the path of sanctification and we still tend to sin. Therefore, we still need to look to the Holy Spirit, who has already worked in our hearts to continue to transform us into the image of Christ. The Holy Spirit will preserve us until the coming of the Lord (Phil 1:6). In this sense, a pure heart is also a promise for us. Only on the last day will purity be fully realized in the glory of Christ.

In this way, a pure heart is a gift of our past as well as a promise for the future. In the present time, it is a mission that we must strive to achieve. Although we have been cleansed by the baptism of Christ and the Holy Spirit, the wounds of original sin in the soul still remain in us. The weakness of the human will and reason still often causes people to worship the creation, including man himself, as an idol. The infatuation with external objects, the body, and the self will still seduce people make their own desires the goal of life. Deep-rooted "sexual immorality, theft, murder, adultery, coveting, wickedness, deceit, sensuality, envy, slander, pride, foolishness" (Mark 7:21–22) still frequently arise, and even become the leading factors in life. Therefore, Christians need to pursue a pure heart. It is a process. It always requires us to remove impurities from our lives. It is a path of spiritual education in which we walk in Christ, with Christ, and through Christ. In this sense, a pure heart is not a state in which we exist but an activity to be pursued.

Such purity of heart stems both from faith and good works; it is both divine grace and human spiritual practice. As St. Benedict puts it, to pray is to work. Faith and good deeds, divine grace and spiritual practice, are inseparable. This requires us to pray constantly in order to purify and improve our good works with the grace of the Holy Spirit. At the same time, we must strive for excellence in our daily practice to cultivate wisdom and discernment, courage to do good, moderation, prudence, and quiet obedience. We need to use these virtues to nourish faith before God. As Augustine said:

> For if God is man's chief good, which you cannot deny, it clearly follows, since to seek the chief good is to live well, that to live well is nothing else but to love God with all the heart, with all the soul, with all the mind; and, as arising from this, that this love must be preserved entire and incorrupt, which is the part of temperance; that it give way before no troubles, which is the part of fortitude; that it serve no other, which is the part of justice; that it be watchful in its inspection of things lest craft or fraud steal in, which is the part of prudence. This is the one perfection of man, by which alone he can succeed in attaining to the purity of truth.[1]

Therefore, for Christians a basic connotation of a pure heart is to be upright, a virtue which steers the soul in the right direction. In answering the questions of the scribes, Jesus identified the two cornerstones of the life of the disciples: "love the Lord your God with all your heart and with all your soul and with all your mind," and "love your neighbor as yourself" (Matt 22:37–39). In Luke 14:33, he more clearly challenged the disciples to love him more than anything or anyone else: "So therefore, any one of you who does not renounce all that he has cannot be my disciple" (Luke 14:33). Such uprightness did not require the disciples to give up or restrain all their emotions and desires, but to guide them correctly. Just like a reservoir, emotions can provide a source of nourishment for a person with a proper life order, but they can also become a flood that destroys everything. Under the guidance of the Holy Spirit, a Christian with an upright heart can direct his whole person, including various subjective emotions—even his pain, fear,

---

1. Augustine, *On the Morals of the Catholic Church*, ch. 25, para. 46.

and sadness—and may become complete in the path towards goodness and love.

There is a mutually reinforcing circle between faith, uprightness, and the pure heart. Christians obey God through faith; in obedience they can live in righteousness; in righteousness they have a clean heart; because their minds are clean, they can better understand what they believe, and thus have stronger faith.

A person who achieves purity is the person who truly knows his or her own nature. The one who is pure in heart will also be the diligent one. The diligent one here is not a person who has exhausted his or her energy through the will, but refers positively to the fact that the person has returned to the state before original sin, to the pure state of the image and likeness of God (Gen 1:26). When a person under the guidance of the Holy Spirit cleanses the soul and frees it from excessive attachment to worldly things, overcoming all kinds of greed and envy, and attains a pure heart, the soul will be able to revert to the image and likeness of God at the beginning of creation. This is what Mencius (372–289 BC) believed: "He who has exhausted all his mental constitution knows his nature. Knowing his nature, he knows Heaven."[2] But this knowledge must be based on the premise of a pure heart; only if the heart has been wiped clean like a mirror from all defilement is it possible to reflect the image of God imprinted on it. As we read in 1 Corinthians 13:12, "For now we see in a mirror dimly, but then face to face." Therefore, Jesus said in the sixth beatitude, "Blessed are the pure in heart, for they shall see God" (Matt 5:8).

The next question is: What does it mean to "see God"? Seeing God has a long tradition in the Old Testament. After the Israelites came out of Egypt and came to Sinai to make a covenant with God and to receive the Ten Commandments and the covenant, they held a confirmation ceremony with God. At that time, the Israelites were in the most intimate relationship with God. The Bible uses the language of "seeing God" to describe this intimacy between people and God: "and they saw the God of Israel. There was under his feet as it were a pavement of sapphire stone, like the very heaven for clearness. And he did not lay his hand on the chief men of the people of Israel; they beheld God, and ate and drank" (Exod 24:10–11).

What is seeing? In the Bible, seeing implies ownership. To see God is to possess God. It means harmony between humanity and God. God not only gave love, happiness, and grace to those who love him, but also gave

---

2. "Chapter of Jinxin I," in Yang Bojun, ed., *Mencius*, 331.

himself as their best and greatest reward. To see God is to see the majesty of God, the beauty of purity and holiness, and to understand his eternal compassion and grace.

To see is the most direct and most vivid experience of the human as he or she lives in the world. Seeing God does not mean that our eyes view an object under light, but that God is the source of light who enlightens us. His holy light can heal our wounds; it can complete our corrupted depravity; it can even make us like the Lord Jesus, as the apostle says, "we know that when he appears we shall be like him, because we shall see him as he is (1 John 3:2)." In three of the Gospels, there is a record of "transfiguration" (Matt 17:1–9; Mark 9:2–8; Luke 9:28–36). The disciples all pointed out that Jesus "was transfigured before them, his face shone like the sun, and his clothes became white as light" (Matt 17:2). The transfiguration of Jesus is typological of the transformation that takes place when a person sees God.

But as the Bible tells us, "you cannot see my face, for man shall not see me and live" (Exod 33:20). Even Moses, who was the friend of God, could see only God's back, but not God's face (Exod 33:23). So how can people "see God"?

A person can stand before God only through a mediator. According to the will of God from before the creation of the world, his son Christ descended into the world in the likeness of a man. The Son is the "the image of the invisible God" (Col 1:15). Christ is the true light that comes from the true light and enjoys the same glory as God. Jesus is the image through whom we can see God. When we see the only Son, we can see the face of God and survive.

The incarnation of Jesus gave us the hope of seeing God and changed the way we see God. In Jesus' face, we see God. Similarly, we also want to see God through the eyes of Jesus. Those who are pure in heart, freed from the obscurity of all material desires, take Jesus as the master of the soul, and they will try to see everything through the eyes of Jesus. They see the image of God in the face of the poor; the poor is like their neighbor. They welcome all people indiscriminately.

Those who are pure in heart are no longer subject to material desires and they never place themselves above the position of the Creator. When they look at nature, they do not regard created things as subjects under their control, or as instruments to satisfy their material desires, but they regard everything as a spiritual partner, through which they can see God. As St. Bonaventure said, "the more we feel the working of God's grace within our hearts, the better we learn to encounter God in creatures outside ourselves."[3] This means that for those who are pure in heart, meeting with God inwardly and encountering God in the outside world are the same. The more they can enjoy the presence of God in their hearts, the more they will be able to enjoy the presence of God in all natural and external opportunities.

Those who are pure in Christ will enjoy the supreme state where, in the words of the apostle Paul, God will be "all in all" (1 Cor 15:28). The first "all" refers to every specific thing, and the second "all" refers to God, who contains everything. Therefore, "all in all" means that all the goodness present in the realities and experiences of this world is present in God eminently and infinitely. Or more properly, in each of these sublime realities is God, as St. John the Cross pointed out in his *Spiritual Canticles*. He did not regard these finite things in the world as sacred things but felt that there was an inner connection between all things and God, so that he encountered God in all things. This is the spiritual experience that St. John of the Cross described: "Mountains have heights, and they are plentiful, vast, beautiful, graceful, bright and fragrant. These mountains are what my Beloved is to me. Lonely valleys are quiet, pleasant, cool, shady and flowing with fresh water; in the variety of their groves and in the sweet song of the birds, they afford abundant recreation and delight to the senses, and in their solitude and silence, they refresh us and give rest. These valleys are what my Beloved is to me."[4] Everything finds its right place in God and God resides in all things. This is the vision of God that the pure in heart will see.

PRAYER

Lord Jesus, you are God's eternal Word, but you were born among us into our world. Our souls rejoice before you, and we call on all the things in the world to jump for joy because God our Lord has come.

Lord, you created in Adam a pure heart in your image and likeness. We pray that you will send your Spirit to cleanse our sinfulness and to keep our hearts pure in your abundant grace.

---

3. Bonaventura, *On the Sentences* 23.2.3, quoted in Pope Francis, *Laudato Si*, 233, 169.

4. John the Cross, *Spiritual Canticle*, 14.6–7.

Lord, you have shown us how to keep a pure heart in facing temptations. We pray that you will purify our hearts with your Word and lead us to dedicate our minds to the one God.

Lord, your incarnation not only redeemed us, but also renewed this earth, which longed for you. Give us a pure heart, and preserve this earth entrusted to us; enable us to see you in all things.

Amen.

20

The Peacemakers

SCRIPTURE

"Blessed are the peacemakers, for they shall be called sons of God." (Matt 5:9)

"For he himself is our peace, who has made us both one and has broken down in his flesh the dividing wall of hostility." (Eph 2:14)

"But the wisdom from above is first pure, then peaceable, gentle, open to reason, full of mercy and good fruits, impartial and sincere. And a harvest of righteousness is sown in peace by those who make peace." (Jas 3:16–18)

QUESTIONS

1. What does peace mean for Christians? Why do we say that God is peace? How is peace engraved in the work of God's creation and redemption? What kind of peace did Jesus accomplish for us?
2. Why does the Bible say that peace is wisdom from above? Explain how peace can be both a gift as well as a task.
3. How may Christians become children of peace? Why do we say that the Son of Peace is also the Son of God?

MEDITATION

In his first sermon, Jesus revealed the way to true happiness in the Beatitudes. The Beatitudes are not only external requirements of an ethical system but are also the internal practice of the soul. It reveals to the followers of Jesus a lofty spiritual realm. This realm reaches a peak in the blessing of the one who brings peace.

The Chinese Union Version translated the seventh beatitude as "people who bring harmony," which is based on a narrower interpretation of the word "peace." When we notice the word "harmony" in the Bible, we should realize that it is the same word as "peace" and "reconciliation." These words can be used interchangeably; they complement each other, indicating that there is a perfect harmony between heaven and people, people and people, and nature and people.

In the Gospel of Luke, at the time of Christmas, the angels and heavenly host sang together, "Glory to God in the highest, and on earth peace among those with whom he is pleased!" (Luke 2:14). "Peace" and "glory" are two words that correspond to each other. This encourages us to meditate on the question: What is the significance of peace in Christian belief?

Peace is an important attribute of God. The Holy Trinity is a peaceful communion. The God of Christian faith is the God of the Holy Trinity. Because of the three persons' mutual love for each other, they are a unity. The communion between them in love makes the Holy Trinity an ocean of peace. Like love, peace is also a name of God. Meditating on the Holy Trinity may bring people the spiritual power to overcome discord.

Firstly, God is peace. According to Philippians 4:7, "And the peace of God, which surpasses all understanding, will guard your hearts and your minds in Christ Jesus." With his peace, God leads and protects the hearts of Christians and keeps all the followers of Jesus united in peace. In Romans 15:33, Paul prays, "May the God of peace be with you all," which shows that peace is not just an object given by God but is an extension of God. God is peace. Secondly, the birth of the Lord Jesus was the birth of peace in the world; as Ephesians 2:14 says, "He himself is our peace." The birth of Jesus not only bridged the gap between humanity and God, it also brought all ethnic groups together in the household of God (Eph 2:19). The peace between people and God and different ethnic groups became a reality in the coming of the Prince of Peace. When Jesus preached to the disciples before his passion, he said, "my peace I give to you" (John 14:27), which means that he does not give the disciples peace as an external thing, but he lets peace flow out of himself into the lives of the disciples. Finally, the Holy Spirit is also the Spirit of Peace. When Jesus came up from the Jordan River when he was baptized, "the Holy Spirit descended on him like a dove" (Luke 3:22). This recalls the image of the dove that brought back an olive branch after Noah's flood to indicate that after the destruction of the world peace had returned (Gen 8:8–9:17). On the night of the resurrection, when Jesus appeared to the disciples, his first words were, "Peace be to you!" Then he breathed out the Holy Spirit of pardon and peace (John 20:21–23). The Holy Spirit works within all of the disciples of Jesus and produces the fruit of peace in their lives (Gal 5:22).

Peace is also engraved in God's creation. When God created the world, the Holy Trinity left his mark in all created things. The God of peace created a peaceful world, but at the same time, just as God has three different persons, this peaceful world inherently contains differences. In this case, peace is not a simple homogeneity. Like the three different persons of the triune God, who form a unity of intrinsic harmony, the world created by God exists in a peaceful union although it is made up of a myriad of things. Therefore, peace here does not merely have a negative connotation regarding the absence of disputes and sin, but positively contains order, vitality, and glory.

As described in the first two chapters of Genesis, the first created world was immersed in the peace of God; the world that God originally created was a world of perfect peace. This peace includes the following aspects. Firstly, everything existed with its uniqueness as well as in an ordered unity. God used the way of separation to create the universe. Heaven, earth, and the sea came into existence. Then these spaces were filled with birds, animals, fish, and people. There was a great variety of things. The world was complex and full of diversity and order. Secondly, all creatures were at peace with each other. After the creation of humans and animals, according to the Genesis account, God said, "Behold, I have given you every plant yielding seed that is on the face of all the earth, and every tree with seed in its fruit. You shall have them for food. And to every beast of the earth and to every bird of the heavens and to everything that creeps on the earth, everything that has the breath of life, I have given every green plant for food" (Gen 1:29–30). Animals did not fear humans (see Gen 9:2). All animals also fed on plants. All creatures lived in peace with one another. There were no carnivorous animals, which is also the kind of environment that the prophet Isaiah hoped for: "The wolf shall dwell with the lamb, and the leopard shall lie down with the young goat, and the calf and the lion and the fattened calf together; and a little child shall lead them. The cow and the bear shall graze; their young shall lie down together; and the lion shall eat straw like the ox. The nursing child shall play over the hole of the cobra, and the weaned child shall put his hand on the adder's den. They shall not hurt or destroy in all my holy mountain; for the earth shall be full of the knowledge of the Lord as the waters cover the sea" (Isa 11:6–9). Thirdly, peace implies a dialectic dynamic between movement and rest. God created the world during the first six days of creation and life rejoiced in heaven and earth. But on the seventh day, "God rested from all his work," and the world entered into a rest. During the first six days, all things moved together and in harmony with each other, and on the seventh day, as a whole, they celebrated the Creator in rest. All things in the world maintained a dynamic peace in the rhythm of movement and rest. Fourthly, the human spirit and body were also in harmony. God first used the dust on the earth to create the human body and humanity was made of dust to show the unity between humanity and the physical world. But God "breathed into his nostrils" and he became "a living soul" (Gen 2:7). This in turn shows that the human soul comes from God and communicates with God through the spirit. Man comes from both the earth and God. Man, as a "living being," has a material body and an immaterial spirit that existed in a state of peace, and thus acted as the bridge or mediator between the whole tangible creation and its intangible Creator. Fifthly, men and women were also at peace. After God created Eve from Adam's rib, he led her to Adam. Adam said, "This at last is bone of my bones and flesh of my flesh; she shall be called Woman, because she was taken out of Man" (Gen 2:23). This shows the oneness between the man and the woman. The man and the woman were mutually the other.

Peace is also the main theme of salvation. Death entered the world through sin. Dissension, corruption, and depravity destroyed God's peace. Therefore, in a word, salvation is the restoration of the peace of God in the world. In the description of salvation history in the Old Testament, several key redemptive events illustrated the Lord's victory over the destructive forces at play in the universe, as described in the Song of Moses after the crossing of the Red Sea in Exodus 15. In the message of prophets, the terms "salvation" and "peace" can be used interchangeably. For example, in Ezekiel 37:26 the new relationship between God and humanity is referred to as "a covenant of peace," and Isaiah 52:7 says, "How beautiful upon the mountains are the feet of him who brings good news, who publishes peace, who brings good news of happiness, who publishes salvation, who says to Zion, 'Your God reigns.'" In traditional Hebrew poetry peace and salvation often appear in parallel construction. The most classic and condensed generalization of "peace" in ancient Israelite tradition is the so-called Aaronic blessing in Numbers 6:24–25: "The Lord bless you and keep you; the Lord make his face to shine upon you and be gracious to you; the Lord lift up his countenance upon you and give you peace." God's blessings, light, protection, and gifts are condensed in God's "peace."

The incarnation of Jesus was the decisive event of salvation history. This was also the highest peak of God's peace coming to earth and humanity. Peace is a gift of God. When Jesus was born, the angels sang, "Glory to God in the highest, and on earth peace among those with whom he is pleased!" (Luke 2:14). Paul also said, "He is our peace" (Eph 2:14). Through Jesus Christ we "have peace with God" (Rom 5:1). Through faith in Jesus, we accepted the gift of peace given by God. And with peace from above, we become ambassadors in this world to transmit peace through our lives, working to realize that original harmonious relationship between God and humanity, between the sexes, and between humanity and the natural environment.

The peace brought about by Jesus is the ultimate peace. Jesus reminded us not to fall into a false and limited peace. In Matthew 10:34–37, he warned the disciples and said, "Do not think that I have come to bring peace to the earth. I have not come to bring peace, but a sword. For I have come to set a man against his father, and a daughter against her mother, and a daughter-in-law against her mother-in-law. And a person's enemies will be those of his own household. Whoever loves father or mother more than me is not worthy of me, and whoever loves son or daughter more than me is not worthy of me." With such vivid language Jesus reminded people that the peace he brings is a true and all-embracing peace, and that the peace that is built around the self, the family, and the nation is nothing but limited peace. People are accustomed to establishing their own self-centered peace, which inevitably leads to a struggle with others. This kind of self-centered peace is based on the premise of attacking others. As the ancient Chinese philosopher Mozi (468–376 BC) once warned, "At present feudal lords have learned only to love their own states and not those of others. Therefore, they do not scruple about attacking other states. The heads of houses have learned only to love their own houses and not those of others. Therefore, they do not scruple about usurping other houses. And individuals have learned only to love themselves and not others. Therefore, they do not scruple about injuring others. When feudal lords do not love one another there will be war on the fields. When heads of houses do not love one another, they will usurp one another's power. When individuals do not love one another, they will injure one another. When ruler and ruled do not love one another they will not be gracious and loyal."[1] This limited peace is selfish and small-scale, and is at the expense of the peace of others, and therefore cannot be long-lasting. Therefore, the establishment of an all-embracing peace in the ultimate sense involves the dissolution of limited peace.

Jesus was God who became a man. He had the same essence and same glory as God, but he took on the shape of a man, entered the created world, and became a part of creation. His purpose was to transform all creation through himself, so that all creation may have peace with God. He had the authority of the Son, was the true God, and was the ruler of the universe. He had the power to bring all creation into harmony with God. As Scripture says, "All things were made through him, and without him was not anything made that was made" (John 1:3). Heaven and earth, the visible and invisible world, all came into being through him. "For by him all things were created, in heaven and on earth, visible and invisible, whether thrones or dominions or rulers or authorities—all things were created through him and for him" (Heb 1:16). "For from him and through him and to him are all things. To him be glory forever" (Rom 11:36). The sonship and divinity of Jesus mean that the peace brought by his incarnation, crucifixion, and resurrection would be the ultimate peace for the whole creation.

Jesus originally had the same perfect reality as God, but through his incarnation and cross he broke himself and poured out his fullness upon the earth, so that all creation may share in his divine nature and glory. He had enjoyed complete peace in the love relationship of the Holy Trinity. However, he used his own actions to end violence and death by means of violence and death, so that the created world could enjoy the peace of God. In Colossians 1:19–22 we read, "For in him all the fullness of God was pleased to dwell, and through him to reconcile to himself all things, whether on earth or in heaven, making peace by the blood of his cross. And you, who once were alienated and hostile in mind, doing evil deeds, he has now reconciled in his body of flesh by his death, in order to present you holy and blameless and above reproach before him."

---

1. Fang Yong, ed., "On Common Love II," in *Mozi*, 125.

The Peacemakers

The eternal peace brought about by Jesus is a gift for humanity because it is realized in the world through the actions of the Son, which consisted in two steps of self-emptying. In Philippians 2:5–8, we find a concise summary of Jesus' salvific work: "Have this mind among yourselves, which is yours in Christ Jesus, who, though he was in the form of God, did not count equality with God a thing to be grasped, but emptied himself, by taking the form of a servant, being born in the likeness of men. And being found in human form, he humbled himself by becoming obedient to the point of death, even death on a cross." The first step in his self-emptying was to become a man; the Creator became a creature. The second step in his emptying of himself was his death on the cross. Incarnation is the premise of the cross, and the cross is the complete realization of the incarnation. To achieve the purpose of incarnation, he had to go to the cross; the suffering and bloodshed on the cross would realize the eternal peace demonstrated by the incarnation. God's grace and love lie behind Jesus' incarnation, death, and resurrection.

Jesus' mention of "peacemakers" in the seventh beatitude refers to himself, but this is also a mission he entrusted to his disciples. For those who want to follow him, to become a peacemaker is what Jesus promised them; it is a goal to be achieved in their life.

Jesus "is our peace" (Eph 2:14). Therefore, since Jesus is Lord, those who want to imitate him should also pursue peace in their lives. They are to be children of peace, ambassadors of peace, and the instruments of peace. They need to live in peace at every level of life.

Jesus' life was a peace offering. The word "offering" from ancient Israelite tradition clearly shows us the way of Jesus' fulfilling God's peace in the world: he offered himself as a sacrifice. Simply put, people of peace are not self-centered. Firstly, they treat others as brothers and partners. This kind of peace is not built on our control over others. Such people regard others, even natural things, as their partners. The meaning of a partner is "I am you, and you are me." Others and all things are another me, and I am another you. This is a kind of peace where the two of us are in a benevolent relationship, and benevolent love is the essence of Christian peace.

Secondly, it is a peace without discrimination. When a person is self-centered, he or she will look at everything around him at a distance and treat others as friends or enemies. But Jesus told us to love our enemies. This means that we must treat everyone the same with no discrimination. Everything reflects the glory of God. This peace does not make discrimination but accepts everything that comes out of the will of God.

Finally, it is a kind of gratuitous goodwill. The peace of Christ is a gift. Likewise, our peace is a gift. It is not an exchange in any kind of transaction, nor is it a reward for what others have done for us, nor is it necessary for others to repay it in the future.

The peace mission that Jesus demands of us is an all-embracing, ultimate peace. This mission includes the task of making no conflict between our fellows, but it is more than that. The scope of the mission is to establish an all-embracing and lasting peace. Jesus asks us, after we have obtained peace with God in Christ, to realize true peace with ourselves, with others, and with nature.

To be a peacemaker, a Christian must first be at peace with himself and be a peaceful person. However, how may one become a peaceful person? On the surface, peace means that there is no war, but inner peace means that we are in a deep harmony with every moment of our lives. We have no complaint with God and no grudge against other people, but are grateful for every moment of life, living in harmony with our surroundings. This peace allows us to live in the moment. In other words, at every moment of life, we are not burdened by what we have, nor are we saddened by what we do not have. This is the so-called way of smoothness promoted in ancient Chinese philosophy. We conform to everything God has arranged for our lives. We believe that God is completely in control over everyone and everything. In this way, we can achieve a truly peaceful life. It allows us to concentrate on our lives and accept each other, neither hanging on to unpleasant memories nor worrying about the future. In this way, we treat each moment as a gift from God and live in it.

Any true inner peace must be closely linked with our concern for the peace of humanity and ecological harmony. Peaceful relations with society and nature are not merely external. They are integrated with our inner peace and enable us to live a full life in the Son of Peace. For us, to restore and maintain peace at the level of human society is to develop a Christian horizon of embracing all humanity, in what is called "in compassion with all under the heaven" (*Tianxia*). Paul said, "For as many of you as were baptized into Christ have put on Christ. There is neither Jew nor Greek, there is neither slave nor free, there is no male and female, for you are all one in Christ Jesus" (Gal 3:27–28). In Christ, we have a peaceful relationship with God and are accepted as children of God. Being children of God is our most fundamental identity, from which we may use a non-discriminatory heart to look at other so-called identities, such as gender, race, class status, and so on. The peace of Christ makes people realize that obsession with such identities is the source of the chaos and war in human society. That obsession leads to gender wars between men and women, class struggles between different classes, and wars between different ethnic groups or nations.

The peace of Christ makes us children of peace. The world is the world of all people; it is not the world of a particular group of people. In Christ, the peace between God and humanity brings humanity and God together in love. The peace between God and humanity is extended to the reality of all human relationships. You and I are united in love; I am you and you are me. According to Confucianism, the character of *ren* (benevolent love) itself is composed of "two" and "people," meaning that benevolent love makes the two into one, and each one becomes a benefactor in the you-me relationship. With further development, people will be able to respect not just themselves but also others; they will care not just for their own families but also for the families of others; they will be concerned not just for their own country but also for other countries.[2] In this way, in the peace of Christ it will be possible to establish world peace by means of righteousness.

We must also extend the peace of Christ to the relationship between humanity and nature. God created heaven and earth, in which the human is only a manager, repairer, and caretaker. The mission of humanity is to lead heaven and earth in all things in harmony to praise God. In this sense, all things in heaven and earth are not merely objects to be controlled but our spiritual friends. However, in modern times, under the domination of rationalism, people have used science and technology as a means to reduce nature to a purely passive object, and, in response to the consumerism-oriented economic system, they increasingly regard everything in the world as objects to be dominated. Viewed as an object, creation can be misused, exploited, and even oppressed. Inspired by scientism, consumerism, and hedonism, humanity has launched a war against heaven and earth. In this war, there are natural scars; animal and plant species are disappearing in an accelerated rate, and the earth is full of holes. The pollution of the atmosphere and water resources is becoming more and more serious. Naturally, the earth is taking its revenge on humanity. Extreme climatic changes have emerged in an endless torrent, and places that are not suitable for human habitation have increased. Even now, humanity and nature are in a fierce

---

2. Hu Pingsheng, and Zhang Meng, eds., "Movement of the Rite," in *Book of Rites*, 419–20.

struggle. "Therefore, the land mourns, and all who dwell in it languish, and also the beasts of the field and the birds of the heavens, and even the fish of the sea are taken away" (Hos 4:3).

In the depths of our lives, Christ has achieved peace. This inner peace also requires us to end our war with nature, restore nature to its role as our spiritual companion, and so realize peace between heaven and earth. God used his powerful word to call heaven and earth into being from nothingness. The existence of all things carries his breath. All things are revealed in God and God fills them in all things. In the creation of all things, "the Lord God formed the man of dust from the ground and breathed into his nostrils the breath of life" (Gen 2:7). Only the human spirit comes directly from the breath of God's own lips. The identity of humanity as the head of all things does not mean that he has the power to dominate everything, but in his capacity as the eldest son of spirituality he discovers the spirituality given by God in all things and leads all things into praise of the Creator.

This will further open our experience of encountering God in both the external and internal dimensions. The more we experience the grace of God in our hearts, the more we will be able to encounter God in external things. In such a spiritual state, we may even say that it does not matter whether our experience is internal or external; internal is external, and external is internal. We may encounter God in both the internal and the external. In a leaf, in a drop of dew, on a footpath, in the face of a child, in the skyline of a church building, in the land where our ancestors were buried, in a faith community that combines daily life, work, and worship together; in all of these we may experience an inner and deep connection between God and them. Everything with its beauty reflects God's appearance.

In this way, based on our peace in Christ, we achieve peace with self, with others, and with heaven and earth. It is also the rest of all things in God. Rest is the peace shared by the Creator and the creation. "And on the seventh day God finished his work that he had done, and he rested on the seventh day from all his work that he had done" (Gen 2:2). What is the purpose of God's creation? It is that all things may find rest in God and glorify him. The seventh day was the last day of creation and it is the only day that is designated as holy. Throughout the first six days, the seventh day was the final destination. This day is a rest and a celebration. In silence and peace, all things are united in the Spirit of God, and together they praise the Creator. The whole universe is immersed in an atmosphere of ultimate harmony and enters the world of peace.

PRAYER

Lord Jesus, when you were born, the angels announced peace to the world. We now celebrate your birth and pray sincerely to you. May your birth bring peace to the world.

Lord Jesus, you willingly left the sanctuary of eternal peace in the Holy Trinity, endured the agony of separation from the Father on the cross, and became our peace offering. We pray you to send the Holy Spirit and make us peacemakers in this world.

Lord Jesus, you are the collector of all weapons, changing the sword into a plough and the spear into a sickle. We pray that you will end all quarrels and disharmony, turn hatred into love and insults into forgiveness.

Lord Jesus, may we in all things, at every moment, meet with you, the Prince of Peace. Lead us to the peace of eternal rest.

Amen.

21

Those Who Are Persecuted for Righteousness

SCRIPTURE

"Blessed are those who are persecuted for righteousness' sake, for theirs is the kingdom of heaven.

Blessed are you when others revile you and persecute you and utter all kinds of evil against you falsely on my account. Rejoice and be glad, for your reward is great in heaven, for so they persecuted the prophets who were before you." (Matt 5:10–12)

"Beloved, do not be surprised at the fiery trial when it comes upon you to test you, as though something strange were happening to you. But rejoice insofar as you share Christ's sufferings, that you may also rejoice and be glad when his glory is revealed. If you are insulted for the name of Christ, you are blessed, because the Spirit of glory and of God rests upon you." (1 Pet 4:12–14)

QUESTIONS

1. What is the difference between the eighth and the previous seven beatitudes?

2. Is there any link between them?

3. How does the eighth blessing remind us of our relationship with the world?

4. What is the relationship between those who are persecuted and the crucified Jesus? How do we and Jesus share in each other's suffering and persecution?

MEDITATION

People do not like persecution, but Jesus' Beatitudes end with persecution as the culmination of true blessing. It is intended to point out that those who are persecuted for righteousness are the true disciples of Jesus, who was crucified. Just as Jesus was crucified on the cross so that people may receive true freedom, the disciples were persecuted in the world, which enabled God's blessing to spread throughout the world. Only in this way could this rebellious and depraved world enter into God's life and blessing.

As the last blessing, the eighth beatitude is special. This is manifested in two aspects. Firstly, the preceding seven blessings mainly fall into the realm of life, personal cultivation, or the intrinsic domain of character, whereas the eighth blessing is related to one's external social relations. It talks about one's relationship with the world around him or her. Secondly, whereas the previous seven blessings were directions for the disciples to take the initiative to pursue, the eighth blessing pointed out to the disciples what the world would impose on them. To put it simply, the first seven blessings focus on personal cultivation, whereas the eighth blessing focus on the way we preserve our faith in an oppressive world. The eighth blessing is the real blessing of action. It reminds us that the blessing of Jesus would be cultivating one's character, but one's cultivation cannot be separated from interaction with the world. It requires us to enter the world, to engage with the concrete issues of everyday life, especially to imitate Jesus in conflicts with the world.

Just as in Jesus' nativity story, after many praised Jesus' glorious identity, the hymn of Simeon pointed out that Jesus would be crucified, so too with the eighth beatitude Jesus calmly told the disciples that the road to blessing was not to be realized by participating in this sinful world. This world is still under the influence of Satan. The blessings that the disciples receive in Jesus consist not only in inner spirit or character, but also in external tensions with this world. Christians are not just to be concerned about themselves; their pursuit of humility, mourning, meekness, compassion, purity of heart, and peace is not something that can be accomplished by separation from this world. To enjoy the true blessing of Jesus the disciples must return to the world and, amid persecution and mistreatment, bring about God's peace and compassion in the world.

If we worship Jesus, who was crucified, will we still refuse to suffer in this world? Will we not accept persecution as God's blessing to us?

In the Gospel of Matthew, the Beatitudes form a special unit. It was the first speech of Jesus' public ministry. It is the key to understanding the gospel of Christ and the epitome of the entire gospel. It is both a set of instructions to the followers of Jesus and a portrayal of Jesus' personal life. From then on, Jesus was no longer the carpenter of Joseph's family. He began to engage with the crowds, not only telling them the truth of the gospel but also walking in the way of the cross. Step by step, he showed us how the Word who became flesh walked in the way of the cross and how he brought salvation to completion. The incarnation and the cross complement each other and mutually interpret each other. The Beatitudes also reflect this structure; the first seven blessings correspond to our rich life in Christ, but such a life needs to be exposed to the world through persecution.

The heart is the seat of blessing and it is where we receive the blessings of Christ. Therefore, the Christian heart does not exist independently. It is formed in our exchanges with Christ. Jesus was the Word who became flesh so that we may live according to the Word in our lives. It was Christ who exchanged his righteousness for our sins. In Christ, we are accepted into God's family and meet with Christ at every moment through prayer. In prayer, we meet with Christ and communicate with him. In the grace of Christ, we are gradually communicating with Christ. Under his illumination, we become more and more like him. This is how we constantly practice making the heart of Jesus our heart (see Phil 2:5).

The heart is also the source of life and the power for action. We relate to the world though our heart. Just as Jesus embraced the world by walking towards the cross, our hearts will also engage with the world through persecution. The engagement of our heart with the world is our action. The heart does not leave the realm of the outside world; there is nothing outside the heart. To cultivate our heart is to act it out. The Christian's cultivation of the heart cannot exist without this world, but the heart is honed through the actions in the world, and the actions are representations of the heart.

Those Who Are Persecuted for Righteousness

"Have this mind among yourselves, which is yours in Christ Jesus" (Phil 2:5); the union of our hearts with Christ can only be accomplished through engaging with the world. The way of Christ is completed on the cross. So too the Christian's heart can be completed only through the persecution of the world.

According to the text in Matthew, the eighth beatitude is made up of two clauses: one sentence emphasizing "Blessed are those who are persecuted for righteousness," and the other emphasizing "Blessed are you when others revile you and persecute you and utter all kinds of evil against you falsely on my account." This prompts us to consider the following question: What is the relationship between being persecuted for the sake of righteousness and being persecuted for the sake of Jesus?

"Righteousness" is an abstract noun, and it is one of the most common words in the Old Testament. It is inseparable from Yahweh's role as judge. He is the ruler of the world, so he governs all things in righteousness. Righteousness is the inner logic of his kingship. "But the Lord sits enthroned forever; he has established his throne for justice, and he judges the world with righteousness; he judges the peoples with uprightness" (Ps 9:7–8). Just as in Mesopotamian myths the king of the universe was described as sitting at the source of the two rivers to manage the world, justice and righteousness are the two rivers that flow from the Lord to nourish and irrigate the world. "Let justice roll down like waters, and righteousness like an ever-flowing stream" (Amos 5:24). The source of righteousness is the ultimate God. He is the creator, the redeemer, and the legislator. Righteousness is God's basic way to govern the world, but it has different manifestations in different aspects of human society: in the relationship between human beings and God, righteousness is to "love the Lord your God with all your heart and with all your soul and with all your mind and with all your strength"; in the relationship between people, the meaning is to "love your neighbor as yourself" (Mark 12:30–31). When dealing with the poor and the Gentiles in society, it means, "When you reap the harvest of your land, you shall not reap your field right up to its edge, neither shall you gather the gleanings after your harvest. And you shall not strip your vineyard bare, neither shall you gather the fallen grapes of your vineyard. You shall leave them for the poor and for the sojourner" (Lev 19:9–10). In the relationship with nature, righteousness means that "the land shall keep a Sabbath to the Lord" (Lev 25:2).

And "Jesus" is a person's name; but through this name Christians established a close personal relationship with the Creator of the universe. Because of this name, they have a special identity, namely, Jesus' disciples. Then we can understand why the eighth beatitude correlates with being persecuted for the sake of righteousness and being persecuted for the sake of Jesus. The expression "for the sake of righteousness" means "for the sake of Jesus," and the expression "for the sake of Jesus" is not an empty slogan, nor a secret code. It is the practice and responsibility of the Christian in society and nature. It is the realization of righteousness in every aspect of the soul, society, and nature. It requires us to practice the responsibilities of the divine law in the Bible when we recognize our identity as the followers of Jesus. On the other hand, when we fight with evil and pursue the realization of righteousness in society and nature, it is not without source, motivation, and direction. Realization of the kingdom of righteousness in the world is driven by the covenantal love—"My beloved is mine, and I am his" (Song 2:16)—that we have formed in the depths of the soul with Jesus.

It is precisely for this reason that Jesus concluded the Beatitudes with the words, "for so they persecuted the prophets who were before you" (Matt 5:12). In this sense, the prophets in the Old Testament may also be called Jesus' disciples, and the disciples of Jesus will also bear the fate of the Old Testament prophets. In Jesus, the Old Testament prophets were integrated with the New Testament disciples. Therefore, the author of Hebrews in the New Testament said, when exploring the history of faith, "Others suffered mocking and flogging, and even chains and imprisonment. They were stoned, they were sawn in two, they were killed with the sword. They went about in skins of sheep and goats, destitute, afflicted, mistreated—of whom the world was not worthy—wandering about in deserts and mountains, and in dens and caves of the earth" (Heb 11:36–38). These people were "persecuted for righteousness' sake" and are also witnesses to those who are persecuted for Jesus.

It is in being persecuted for the sake of righteousness and for the sake of Jesus that the Christian witnesses that he or she does not belong to this world. In the second century AD, early Christians wrote in a letter describing their calling to be persecuted:

> For Christians are no different from other people in terms of their country, language, or customs. Nowhere do they inhabit cities of their own, use a strange dialect, or live life out of the ordinary. They have not discovered this teaching of theirs through reflection

or through the thought of meddlesome people, nor do they set forth any human doctrine, as do some. They inhabit both Greek and barbarian cities, according to the lot assigned to each. And they show forth the character of their own citizenship in a marvelous and admittedly paradoxical way, by following local customs in what they wear and what they eat and in the rest of their lives. They live in their respective countries, but only as resident aliens; they participate in all things as citizens, and they endure all things as foreigners. Every foreign territory is a homeland for them, every homeland is foreign territory. They marry like everyone else and have children, but they do not expose them once they are born. They share their meals but not their sexual partners. They are found in the flesh but do not live according to the flesh. They live on earth but participate in the life of heaven. They are obedient to the laws that have been made, and by their own lives they supersede the laws. They love everyone and are persecuted by all. They are not understood and they are condemned. They are put to death and made alive. They are impoverished and make many rich. They lack all things and abound in all things. They are dishonored and they are exalted in their dishonors. They are slandered and they are acquitted. They are reviled and they bless, mistreated and they bestow honor. They do good and are punished as evil; when they are punished they rejoice as those who have been made alive. They are attacked by Jews as foreigners and persecuted by Greeks.[1]

Being persecuted in the world is the mark of the true disciple. Their persecution demonstrates that their Lord suffered on the cross and it is precisely the blessing that the disciples receive from Jesus.

But the experience of being persecuted, abused, and vilified is not the end of our life in Christ, just as the suffering of the cross was not the end of Christ's life. Therefore, in the eighth blessing, Jesus encouraged those who are being persecuted to rejoice because their reward would be great in heaven. Persecution, insults, and defamation are only external encounters. Rejoicing is the inner experience of real life.

Why should we rejoice in persecution? Because it is in persecution that we interact with Jesus. This interaction is twofold. In persecution, we participate in the crucifixion of Jesus. At the same time, the suffering Jesus also participates in our persecution. In the famous story of Saul's call on the Damascus road, people usually pay more attention to the light from heaven and ignore the dialogue between Saul and Jesus. There was a voice saying

---

1. *Letter to Diognetus*, in Ehrman, ed., *Apostolic Fathers*, 139–41.

to Saul, "Saul, Saul, why are you persecuting me?" Saul responded, "Who are you, Lord?" Then the Lord said, "I am Jesus, whom you are persecuting" (Acts 9:4–5). Here, instead of saying, "Why are you persecuting my disciples?" the Lord Jesus said, "Why are you persecuting me?" It shows that the persecution of the disciples is precisely the persecution of Jesus himself; in the persecution of the disciples Jesus is the suffering one. The connection between Jesus and his disciples is not weakened in persecution but becomes stronger. The disciples are in him and are also persecuted because of him; he is also in them and is persecuted by the world. Jesus once experienced the suffering of the cross in his flesh. Similarly, he also continues to experience suffering through true disciples. Where the disciples suffer, there is Jesus.

Christian life becomes complete in the participation of Jesus' life. Every Christian life is the reenactment of Jesus' life. This is the meaning of "Christ who lives in me" (Gal 2:20). The life of Jesus was a life in which the archetype of the incarnation, the death on the cross, and the resurrection from the tomb took place. To understand our lives through Jesus is to realize the meaning of these prototypical events for us. At the same time, the life of Jesus is a whole, and so we cannot just treat them as isolated fragments; each event is included in the other events. The incarnated Jesus needed to go through the experience of the cross to fulfill his mission of salvation; likewise, the cross of death, because of his resurrection, became a symbol of glory and victory, and thus his incarnation achieved the ultimate peace for the universe.

In this way the cross, in the context of the incarnation and the resurrection, is not a tragic cross but a jubilant cross. When we come to the cross, we not only come with deep sorrow for the man from Nazareth, but also come with deep love for the king who has triumphed over death. The cross is a symbol of sacrifice, but also of life, love, and hope. In fact, in the tradition of the Eastern church, the cross was presented in the form of four flowers. Indeed, the cross is no longer a horrible instrument of punishment but rather an instrument of abundant life, like budding flowers.

With this view of the cross, we can have a better understanding of the command that Jesus gave to those under persecution: "Rejoice and be glad" (Matt 5:12). When we suffer with Christ, we can rejoice when his glory is revealed (1 Pet 4:13). To be persecuted with Jesus is our joy and happiness, just as the cross is the flower of our life. Persecution also enables us to understand the mystery of Jesus' life more clearly: Jesus defeated death with his death, he defeated suffering with his suffering, and he defeated persecution with his persecution. Since we are linked to such a Lord of life, everything that we encounter in our lives will be transformed and will ascend with Jesus.

Compared with the teachings of the preceding seven blessings, Jesus' teaching in the eighth blessing consists of many layers of meaning, with a melody of ups and downs. The eighth blessing contains a warning: the life of Jesus' disciples will not be only serene and calm. But in the tempering of the world, even in the persecution of the world, the disciples will practice making the heart of Christ their own (see Phil 2:5). The eighth blessing also contains an encouragement: it encourages us to look up at the flowers of life on the cross, and to maintain a joyful heart in the midst of persecution. The eighth blessing also contains a promise: Jesus promised himself to us. In persecution, he participates in our lives. He suffers with us. It reminds us that persecution and suffering are Jesus' blessings. To suffer the persecution is not a stepping-stone for heaven, but it is really a token that we have been accepted as the people of heaven.

PRAYER

Lord Jesus, you are our king. You have come to earth that we may participate in your divine nature. We pray that we will glorify you through our faith and good deeds all of life.

Lord, you were born in a manger and in humility you became one of us. We pray that through your birth we would welcome your glorious kingdom in our humility.

Lord, you took on the form of a human being and revealed your great power through your suffering and resurrection. We pray that we may live out our lives in your great power and rejoice in suffering.

Lord, you lived out the eight Beatitudes in your life, and became a model for our lives. May you live in our hearts forever, that we may live out our life along the way of the Beatitudes.

Amen.

Epilogue
How May Christmas Be Completed?

The incarnation of Christ is the greatest event in human history because it is the peak of God's action in the world and the source of salvation for everyone once and for all eternity. Therefore, theologically, Christ's birth is not a one-off event. It runs throughout God's plan of redemption for the entire created world. So, for every one of us, how may Christmas be completed?

Christ's birth is historically a one-off; he was born in Bethlehem more than two thousand years ago. However, after Christ's ascension into heaven, he continually breathes out his life-giving Holy Spirit and creates divine life in us. Through the everlasting Holy Spirit, Christ is unceasingly born in every soul willing to follow him. Christ was born into our lives and became our life. In this sense, Christmas has not been completed. It is an endless process.

The essence of Christmas is birthing. We are born in Christ and Christ will be born in us. Through the birth of Christ as a person, we have received an eternal new life; that is, we share in God's divine life. The other aspect of this life is that Christ is born in us. Therefore, in the Christian tradition, a metaphor was developed that compares our heart to that of a woman. Our heart is like a woman, but she has two images. Firstly, our heart is like a bride, to be united with Christ as the bridegroom; secondly, our heart is like a mother, sharing spiritually in the privilege of Mary. Under the power of the Holy Spirit, Christ is born into our heart. Only after Christ is born within our birth will he live his life within us, and thus the mystery of Christmas will fulfill its mission.

In this way, the true meaning of the mystery of Christmas is that the life of Christ will be lived out in us. In fact, it is Christ who is living

Epilogue

everything out in us. The purpose of the Father sending the Son is to make the heart of Christ our heart. Today, we participate in Christ's birth to make our heart become Christ's heart.

The advent of Christ and the entire Christmas period, with birthing as the core, remind us to welcome the ever-birthing God and to nourish the life of Christ within us. As the ancient church father Origen said, "He who is begotten by God is always blessed. For I will not say that the righteous man is begotten just once by God, but that he is always begotten in each good act in which God begets the righteous man. If then I set before you, with respect to the Savior, that the Father has not begotten the Son and then severed him from his generation, but always begets him, I will also present something similar for the righteous man."[1] Constant renewal in the Holy Spirit is our constant regeneration in Christ.

In the coming season, we proceed from the subject of hope, preparation, and joy to meditate on Scripture's testimony to Jesus' birth; but in the end, we implement the meditation on Jesus' Beatitudes. This is because the Beatitudes are not only a set of instructions that Jesus gave us but also a description of his own life. The Beatitudes are the full realization of Jesus' human life under the illumination and nourishment of Jesus' divine life. The way of the Beatitudes is the complete unfolding of the purpose of Jesus' birth and it is also the rule of life that we should pursue.

Through the way of the Beatitudes, we walk toward Christ himself, because the Beatitudes contain the faces of Christ's life. In this way, we are heading towards the fountain of eternal life.

Indeed, this way is life.

---

1. Origen, *Homilies on Jeremiah*, IX 4.4, 92.

Bibliography

Anselm. *Complete Philosophical and Theological Treatises of Anselm of Canterbury.* Translated by Jasper Hopkins and Herbert Richardson. Minneapolis: Arthur J. Banning, 2000.

Augustine. *On the Morals of the Catholic Church.* Translated by Richard Stothert. In *Nicene and Post-Nicene Fathers*, ser. 1, vol. 4., edited by Philip Schaff. Buffalo, NY: Christian Literature, 1887.

Brother Lawrence. *The Practice of the Presence of God: The Best Rule of Holy Life.* Edited by Anthony Uyl. Woodstock, ON: Devoted, 2018.

Brother Leo of Assisi. *The Mirror of Perfection: Being a Record of Saint Francis of Assisi.* Translated by Constance Countess de La Warr. London: Burns and Oats, 1902.

Cantalamessa, Raniero. *Beatitudes: Eight Steps to Happiness.* Translated by Marsha Daigle-Williamson. Cincinnati: Servants, 2009.

Catholic Church. *Catechism of The Catholic Church.* New York: Doubleday, 1995.

———. *Liturgy of the Hours.* Vol. 1, *Advent Season and Christmas Season.* New York: Catholic Book, 1975.

Chen Xiaofen, and Xu Ruzong, eds. *Analects* (Lun Yu*), Great Learning* (Da Xue) *and Mean* (Zhong Yong). Beijing: Zhonghua, 2015.

Cyprian of Carthage. *On the Unity of the Church.* Translated by Robert Ernest Wallis. In *Ante-Nicene Fathers*, edited by Alexander Roberts, James Donaldson, and A. Cleveland Coxe, vol. 5. Buffalo, NY: Christian Literature, 1886.

Ehrman, Bart D., ed. *The Apostolic Fathers.* Cambridge, MA: Harvard University Press, 2003.

Fang Yong, ed. "On Common Love II" (Jian Ai II). In *Mozi.* Beijing: Zhonghua, 2015.

Feduccia, Robert, ed. "Selections from *The Story of a Soul.*" In *Great Catholic Writings: Thought, Literature, Spirituality, Social Action.* Winona, MN: Saint Mary's, 2006.

Gardner, D. K., trans. *Learning to Be a Sage: Selections from Conversations of Master Chu.* Berkeley: University of California Press, 1990.

Gregory of Nyssa. "The Beatitudes, 1." In *Ancient Christian Writers*, edited by Johannes Quasten and Joseph C. Plumpe, translated by Hilda C. Graef, vol. 18. Westminster, MD.: Newman, 1954.

Hu Pingsheng, and Zhang Meng, eds. "Movement of the Rite" (Li Yun). In *Book of Rites* (Liji). Beijing: Zhonghua, 2017.

Hunsinger, George. *The Beatitudes.* New York: Paulist, 2015.

Job, Rueben, P., and Norman Shawchuck, eds. *A Guide to Prayer for All Who Seek God.* Nashville: Upper Room, 2006.

Bibliography

John of the Cross. *A Spiritual Canticle of the Soul and the Bridegroom Christ*. Translated by David Lewis, with corrections and introduction by Benedict Zimmerman. St. Luke's, Wincanton, Somerset, 1909. https://jesus-passion.com/SPIRITUAL_CANTICLE.htm.

Lao-Tzu. *Tao Teh King*. Translate by J. Legge. Sacred Books of the East 39. Oxford: Clarendon, 1891.

Legge, James, trans. *The Chinese Classics*. Vol. 1. Hong Kong: Hong Kong University Press, 1960.

Liu Xiang. "A Conversation between Confucius and Zi Gong." In *Garden of Stories* (Shuo Yuan), edited by Xiang Zonglu. Beijing: Zhonghua, 1987.

Origen. *Homilies on Jeremiah and 1 Kings 28*. Translated by John Clark Smith. Washington, DC: Catholic University of America Press, 1998.

Pope Francis. "The Grace of Shame." Morning meditation, chapel of the *Domus sanctae marthae*, March 21, 2017. http://www.vatican.va/content/francesco/en/cotidie/2017/documents/papa-francesco-cotidie_20170321_the-grace-of-shame.html.

———. *Laudato Si* ("On Care for Our Common Home"). Encyclical letter. Rome, May 24, 2015. http://www.vatican.va/content/francesco/en/encyclicals/documents/papa-francesco_20150524_enciclica-laudato-si.html.

Ratzinger, Joseph (Pope Benedict XVI). *Jesus of Nazareth: From the Baptism in the Jordan to the Transfiguration*. New York: Doubleday, 2007.

Ricci, Matteo. "Treatise on Friendship." In *Collection of Chinese Writings of Matteo Ricci* (*Li Ma Dou Zhong Wen Zhu Zuo Yi Ji*). Shanghai: Fudan University Press, 2001.

Roberts, Alexander, and James Donaldson, eds. *The Writings of Irenaeus*. Vol. 1. Translated by Alexander Roberts and W. H. Rambaut. Ante-Nicene Christian Library 5. Edinburgh: T. & T. Clark, 1878.

Rotelle, John E., ed. *The Works of Saint Augustine: A Translation for the 21st Century. Part 3, Sermons 6, (184–229Z) on the Liturgical Seasons*. Translation and notes by Edmund Hill. New Rochelle, NY: New City, 1993.

Tang Zhangping, and Wang Chaohua, eds. *Dao De Jing* (Lao Zi). Beijing: Zhonghua, 2014.

Tertullian. *On Prayer*. Translated by S. Thelwall. In *Ante-Nicene Fathers*, edited by Alexander Roberts, James Donaldson, and A. Cleveland Coxe, vol. 3. Buffalo, NY: Christian Literature, 1887.

Thomas Aquinas. *Summa Theologica*. Translated by Fathers of the English Dominican Province. New York: Benziger, 1911–1925.

Wang Yangming. *Inquiry into the Great Learning*. In *Complete Collection of Wang Yangming*, edited by Wu Guang. Shanghai: Shanghai Ancient Books, 1992.

Yang Bojun, ed. *Mencius*. Beijing: Zhonghua, 2012.

Zhang Zai. *Words on the West Wall* (Xi Ming). In *Collections of Zhang Zai* (Zhang Zai Ji). Beijing: Zhonghua (Zhong Hua Shu Ju), 1978.

Zhou Dunyi. *Penetrating the Book of Changes* (Zhou Zi Tong Shu). Shanghai: Shanghai Ancient Books (Shanghai Gu Ji Chu Ban She), 2000.

Zhu Xi. *Zhu Xi's Conversations* (Zhu Zi Yu Lei). In *Collection of Sage Zhu's Writings* (Zhu Zi Wen Ji), edited by Guo Qi and Yi Bo. Chengdu: Sichuan Education (Si Chuan Jiao Yu Chu Ban She), 1996.

www.ingramcontent.com/pod-product-compliance
Lightning Source LLC
Chambersburg PA
CBHW070448090426
42735CB00012B/2486